LET'S TALK ABOUT SEX

Let's Talk About Sex

A Straightforward Guide for Today's Generation

Larry Tomczak

VINE BOOKS

Servant Publications
Ann Arbor, Michigan

Vine Books is an imprint of Servant Publications especially designed to serve Evangelical Christians.

Published by Servant Books
P.O. Box 8617
Ann Arbor, Michigan 48107

Printed in the United States of America
ISBN 0-89283-353-X
87 88 89 90 91 10 9 8 7 6 5 4 3 2 1

Contents

Foreword

"WHAT'S WRONG with two people sleeping together or living together if they really love each other and are open and honest?" "Not sex with anybody, but what about sex in a *meaningful* relationship?" "What if we have sex, enjoy it, and discover it makes us love each other all the more?" "Are you suggesting I be some kind of prude and say 'no' to sex just because I'm single?" "Haven't times changed?" "Isn't a lot of this talk about herpes and AIDS just a scare tactic and not relevant to those of us who run in straight crowds?"

Good questions deserve honest answers. For everyone who is ready to listen—*let's talk about sex.*

I trust this book will help you become all God intends for you to be.

Sincerely,
Larry Tomczak

Introduction

> God saw everything that He had made, and behold, it was very good. (Gen 1:31 TAB)
>
> Male and female he created them, and he blessed them. (Gen 5:2 RSV)

Many Christians are ashamed to discuss what God is not ashamed to create. Our archenemy seems to have engineered a conspiracy of silence on the subject of sex. As a result, millions of young people are left with confusion and uncertainty.

Keeping pure prior to marriage is like having a 400-horsepower engine in a VW body. Without frank and forthright guidance and supernatural assistance, one is almost destined for a crash.

With so many "sexperts" and sexologists expounding their "wisdom," we need to listen to what the Great Physician, Jesus, has to say. His manual is the greatest best seller ever published. His credentials are most impressive.

> . . . Christ, in whom are hid all the treasures of wisdom and knowledge. (Col 2:3 RSV)

His impact upon crowds is worthy of note.

> And when Jesus finished these sayings, the crowds were astonished—(Greek, exceedingly and abundantly flattened out)—at his teaching. (Matt 7:28 RSV)

He declared while he was with us on earth, "Heaven and earth will pass away, but my words will never pass away" (Matt 24:35 RSV).

Recently an article appeared in a national women's publication ridiculing Christian books and seminars centered around a wife's role in the home. The so-called "expert" who wrote it had brushed aside such teaching as having no real validity in a marriage. Later someone wrote the magazine's editor asking how this expert's marriage fared. The terse reply: "She is twice divorced."

Let's not be ripped off!

Let's not be deceived by the "behavior and customs of this world" which lead to inevitable misery and defeat.

Let's dare to be different and "learn from our own experience how his ways will really satisfy."

Regardless of what we've heard (or not heard), let's go forward with an open mind allowing Jesus to speak to us through his Word.

"How can a young man keep his way pure? By guarding it according to thy word" (Ps 119:9 RSV).

Let's talk about sex.

> And so, dear brothers, I plead with you to give your bodies to God. Let them be a living sacrifice, holy—the kind he can accept. When you think of what he has done for you, is this too much to ask? Don't copy the behavior and customs of this world, but be a new and

different person with a fresh newness in all you do and think. Then you will learn from your own experience how his ways will really satisfy you. (Rom 12:1-2 TLB)

ONE

Getting It Together

AT THE END OF TIME, billions of people were scattered on a great plain before God's throne. Some of the groups near the front talked heatedly—not with cringing shame, but with belligerence.

"How can God judge us? What a rip-off! How can he know about suffering?" snapped a cynical brunette; she jerked back a sleeve to reveal a tattooed number from a Nazi concentration camp. "We endured terror, beatings, torture, death!"

In another group, a black man lowered his collar. "What about this?" he demanded, showing an ugly rope burn. "Lynched for no crime but being black. We have suffocated in slave ships, been wrenched from loved ones, tolied till only death gave release."

Far out across the plain were hundreds of such oppressed minorities. Each had a complaint against God for the evil and suffering he permitted in the world. How lucky God was to live in heaven where there was no oppression. All was sweetness and light. No weeping, no fear, no hunger, no hatred. Indeed, what did God know about the hassles man had in the world? "After all, God leads a pretty sheltered life."

So each group sent out a leader, chosen because he had suffered the most. There was a Jew, a black, an Untouchable from India, an illegitimate son, a prisoner of war, an Indian, and one from a Siberian slave camp. In the center of the plain they consulted with each other. At last they were ready to present their case. It was rather simple—before God would be qualified to be their judge, he must endure what they had endured. Their decision was that God "should be sentenced to live on earth—as a man!"

But, because he was God, they set certain safeguards to be sure he could not use his divine powers to help himself:

1. Let him be born a Jew.
2. Let the legitimacy of his birth be doubted, so that none will know who his father really is.
3. Let him champion a cause so just, but so radical, that it brings down upon him the hate, condemnation and eliminating efforts of the "establishment" and every major traditional and established religious authority.
4. Let him be the object of put-downs and ridicule, be spat upon, labeled "demon" and "mad."
5. Let him try to describe what no man has ever seen, touched, heard, or smelled—let him try to communicate God.
6. Let him be betrayed by his dearest friends.
7. Let him be indicted on false charges, tried before a prejudiced jury, and convicted by a cowardly judge.
8. Let him experience what it is to be terribly alone and completely abandoned by every living thing.
9. Let him be tortured and let him die! Let him die the

most humiliating death—with common thieves.
10. And let his name live on so that for centuries it will be used as a common curse word in moments of rage.

As each leader announced his portion of the sentence, loud murmurs of approval went up from the great throng of people. When the last had finished pronouncing sentence, there was a long silence. No one uttered another word. No one moved. For suddenly they all knew—God has already served his sentence.

"But why?"

Because he loves you.

His cross, wherever displayed, remains an historical monument to this fact. "For God so greatly loved and dearly prized the world that He [even] gave up His only-begotten (unique) Son, so that whoever believes in (trusts, clings to, relies on) Him shall not perish—come to destruction, be lost—but have eternal (everlasting) life" (John 3:16 TAB).

He also wants you to get it together in every part of your life. Not just in the area of sex but in everything. Jesus put it this way, "I am come that they might have life, and that they might have it more abundantly" (John 10:10 KJV).

"But who's living like *that?*"

Very few. Most people have stiff-armed God's love and chosen to live independently of him (even many attending church buildings!). This is what the Bible calls "selfishness" or "sin."

There are only two kingdoms in this world (Col 1:13). Jesus also called them "paths"—a wide one and a narrow one (Matt 7:13-14). You, like everyone else, are in one or the other. There are no other options. Just two—the kingdom of darkness and the kingdom of light. In the kingdom of darkness (named this because those who are in it don't even know it!) there is a governing principle—"*My* will be done." Self is on the throne of a person's life in this kingdom. It's called "doing my own thing." Instead of doing what the Word of God teaches, a person will follow the philosophy: "If it feels good—do it!"

This sounds inviting at first but the results are disastrous.

If you're living by the principle "*my* will be done" and others live by the same principle, eventually wills are going to conflict. The results—war, fighting, riots, divorce, conflict between blacks and whites, Jews and Arabs, men and women, labor and management, faculty and students, parents and kids.... Why do you think the world is in such a mess?

In the other kingdom—the kingdom of light—there's a different governing principle: "*Thy* will be done." People in this kingdom have stepped off the throne—the control center of their lives—and let Jesus be Lord as they walk according to His Word. ("Lord" means "supreme in authority, one in control.") If you're saying, "*Thy* will be done" and I'm saying "*Thy* will be done," harmony, order, and peace will result.

Two thousand years ago people said: "We will not have this man to reign over us!" (Luke 19:14 KJV). The overwhelming majority say the same thing today.

You may have heard the story about the father of a five-year-old boy who was working at home in his study while his wife had gone out for a few hours. It was raining, so his son couldn't play outside. Every few minutes the child would get bored and would come into his dad's study to ask him to play. But the father had too much work, so he had to think of some way to keep his son amused. He finally hit on an idea. He tore a picture of a map of the world out of a magazine, ripped it up into little pieces, and said, "Here, son; go put the world back together again."

His son went into another room and began working on the map. Dad figured he had a few hours of uninterrupted work ahead of him, but in less than a half hour, the boy was back, with the pieces of the picture of the world all back in the right places.

The father couldn't believe his son had put the picture back together so quickly, so he asked him how he did it. The boy said, "It wasn't tough at all, dad. You see, on the back side of the picture of the world was a picture of a man. And when I got the man all straightened out, the world was okay too!"

How about you? Have you gotten things straightened out? It all depends on which kingdom you're in.

"But what about other religions, Eastern philosophy, T.M.?"

There is a legend about a young man who was caught in a bed of quicksand. Confucius saw him and remarked, "There is evidence men should stay out of such places." Buddha came by and said, "Let that life be a lesson to the rest of the world." Mohammed said about the man, "Alas, it is the will of Allah." Maharishi smiled and whispered, "Just meditate—problems recede into oblivion." The Hindu said to him, "Cheer up, friend, you will return to earth in another form." But when Jesus saw him, he said, "Give me your hand, young man, and I will pull you out."

Seventeen years ago I extended that outstretched hand. Stuck on an endless treadmill, I searched in athletics, rock, and booze. Yet I couldn't pull my life together. A void continued to grow inside me.

In high school I worshiped muscles. I looked on enviously when the congested corridors at school quickly parted as a six-foot-two and two-hundred-eighty-five pound football player strode by. Everyone stepped aside so as not to obstruct his path. He had power. He commanded attention. I would watch the football team practice admiring their strength, size, and success, feeling like a grape next to a mass of watermelons.

Soon I had my own set of 220-pound weights (which was 120 pounds more than I could use) and began the "Bob Hoffman Body Building Course." In my bedroom I pasted up pictures from the latest issues of *Mr. America;* mounted inspirational quotes like "When the going gets tough, the tough get going" on my mirror; and daily drank a quart of "Quick Weight-Gain Formula." I ate more, swallowed handfuls of vitamins, and made health foods an integral part of my diet.

For six months I worked out for an hour and a half every other day. My routine began with measuring the expansion of my biceps, neck, chest, and legs. I was determined to add at least two inches to each area.

Every hour of my intense discipline paid off when I heard affirming words from a fellow in the locker room who was changing his clothes next to me. "Hey, you been working out lately?"

"What?" I pretended not to hear.

"I asked if you have been working out. Your arms are getting bigger."

"Wow! It's starting to show!" I thought. I left with renewed determination and jogged all the way home eager to add five more repetitions to each exercise.

In time my devotion shifted from body building to rock and roll. The Mr. America posters were replaced by portraits of rock idols garbed in wild costumes, legs apart, faces in an agony of travail. My room was my one private enclave adorned to reflect my world. Stacks of albums and photographs of the latest heavy metal bands expressed the passion of my interest. When I shut myself in my room, I imagined myself in an amphitheater as the star celebrity clad in black leather, posied for action under the main spotlight. As I closed my eyes, I mouthed the words coming from my stereo and saw myself performing before a vast, appreciative audience. "C'mon baby light my fire." The fantasy enveloped me.

My parents thought my room a "fool's paradise." "Larry! Larry! Do you have to play that noise so loud?"

"You can't feel it unless it's loud," I shouted back. "I've got to hear the drums, and I can't pick them out unless the volume is up."

"Listen here young man, as long as you're in our house, turn it down!"

Jumping from the bed, I'd utter a stream of obscenities while lowering the volume.

Withdrawing my entire life savings of nine hundred and three dollars, I purchased one of the finest sets of drums on the market. My new, gray-ripple, dual-tom, dual-cymbal set of Rogers drums was to be my key to prosperity. My parents were bitterly antagonistic, to say the least.

"Larry! Stop that stupid pounding," my mother

would scream. "I can't stand it anymore! Stop it, or I'll smash those drums!"

Furious, I would slam down my drumsticks or fling them at the wall, clench my fists, jump off my seat, and fly into a rage. I resented any obstacle put in my way.

My need to be somebody was slowly but surely being satisfied. My ego was continually shooting up, while the void seemed to be steadily diminishing. I had joined a rock band and was on my way to stardom. "The Lost Souls" band meant being on stage—with hundreds of adulating eyes looking up to me. I now had money and fame and women. My ego feasted on the whispers I heard when I walked into McDonald's, "Hey, look there. That's one of The Lost Souls."

Going to church simply was not congruent with my lifestyle, and I let one of the church leaders I knew in on my views.

"I've got to level with you. I resent having been indoctrinated into a church that seems so hypocritical and shallow—and, frankly, meaningless." I waited to see the priest's shocked response, but he just looked intently at me. I went on.

"Look around at the guys in this school. We all came here from our little parochial schools, having naively and fearfully accepted everything the teachers taught us. Then, all the freshman year, we were told that we weren't kids any more—no one was going to hold our hand or wipe our nose. We were told to start thinking for ourselves." I slapped the arm of my chair.

"And so we started doing just that, asking questions and looking for reality, not fantasy. But as soon as we'd ask a question about something in the Catholic Church, we were given the fast runaround. 'Because the Church says so, that's why!' Have you any idea how many kids in this school are either atheists or agnostics and how many could care less about going to church?"

Father Sommer looked me in the eye and spoke without smiling. "I think I do, Larry. I've talked to enough of the group to know what you're saying is true. I also know that hundreds of you guys are getting bombed on weekends, and a few of you are beginning to mess around with marijuana, because you're searching for peace and purpose in life, and you're not finding them in the church, so you're looking in the world."

Yes, I believed the world held much promise for me. Midway through my freshman year The Lost Souls secured an engagement for an open-air rock concert in the eighty-thousand-seat Cleveland Municipal Stadium. It all seemed absolutely unreal—The Lost Souls performing a concert in one of the three largest stadiums in the United States. My dream materialized.

Instantly, the public address system of the stadium echoed, *"Ladies and gentlemen, let's welcome The Lost Souls!"*

Springing from the dugout, the five of us darted across the playing field toward the stage. The thunderous reception was deafening; the exaltation made every single minute of practice worthwhile.

"Oh, God, don't let me trip," I pleaded as I approached the stage.

Taking the steps two at a time, I stopped the moment my feet were firmly on the platform. In nonchalant fashion, I sauntered across the stage to my drums, grabbed my set of drumsticks, and sat down, poised for action. Lifting my eyes to the crowd for the first time, I felt a wild chill shoot through my body. Every fantasy I had ever had was realized in that instant. And it was better—it was real. In supreme ecstasy, I sat on my percussion throne, and knew that every eye in Cleveland Stadium was focused on me.

For the next twenty-five minutes, I was in bliss. As the electric guitars vibrated the powerful amplifiers, I helped to build each crescendo with rolling explosions of drum bursts and crashing cymbals. Caught in the spell of raw, base emotion unleashed and translated to the semblance of a melodic line, the youthful audience began to sway with the rhythm and lose themselves increasingly in each song. Some were completely gone, possessed, dancing on their seats or in the aisles, jerking insanely to the frenzy of the electrically charged sounds. And I was the dancemaster, the drumstick my baton. So this was power.

Ironically, within the year, The Lost Souls band were no more. When it happened, I simply could not believe it. My senses seemed disconnected, the malaise affecting my body was so intense that even my breathing was impaired.

How could we all just abandon everything? I thought. The thousands of practice hours, the thousands of dollars invested in our instruments and the amps and the van, the hundreds of promotional pictures, the record, all the clothing . . . the money . . . the recognition. . . .

The debacle of The Lost Souls was not the result of one altercation. Numerous problems had been snowballing for months. The record had failed to galvanize the area promoters. Waning interest in taking the music seriously combined with a contented complacency with the progress in the group. And personality clashes had become bitter and frequent. When Denny Carleton announced that he was quitting, the inscription on the tombstone was clear.

"Well," I said with a sigh, "it had to happen sooner or later." Although my remark sounded calmly resigned, I was unable to repress the surge of grief welling up in my heart. Once back in my room, I closed my eyes and surrendered. The spotlight had gone out.

By my sophomore year at CSU booze had become my means to escape from the growing void within me. I drank heavily on weekends. Buying a six-pack of beer and a bag of chips and then driving my girl to a secluded parking lot was my primary form of amusement.

The effect of beer never lasted long enough, though. After every drinking spree, I still had to face myself in the bathroom mirror as I came back to reality. And each time it got worse.

One night after a good dose of reality, I opened a Bible. It was 2:45 AM when I finished the Gospel of John. Leaning back in my chair, I closed my eyes to hold back the tears welling up. Turning out the light, I sat in a sea of quiet darkness and began to whisper a prayer.

"God, it's been so long since I've really talked to you. I'm sorry. Yet somehow it's all different tonight. All my life I've felt that you were high and holy and unreachable; that's why I gave up on you. And now I see that all my life you've been waiting for me to realize how much you loved me. Oh, Jesus, I want your love . . . I will come unto you. Please, help me, Jesus . . . please."

And I wept—like I hadn't since I was a little child.

I can't remember how long I sat in the darkness. When my tears subsided, a deep sense of peace settled over me, a peace so perfect I hardly dared to breathe. In my heart I knew God had heard me. Somehow everything had changed, for there in the darkness he was with me.

I whispered his name—and grinned, knowing that he heard. I did it again. He seemed to want me to give him the hurts in my life, and like a kid reaching into the toy box to show a loving father one broken toy after another, for him to make them whole, I put them in his hands.

Then I wanted to tell him about the very worst sins I had committed and ask him to forgive me. I did, and he did. And I felt clean, all the way through my being—for the first time in my life.

"Jesus, Jesus, Jesus..." I shook my head, and the tears came again—tears of joy. I was beginning to know the wonder of his love.

> ...I am the bread of life; he who comes to me shall not hunger, and he who believes in me shall never thirst. (John 6:35 RSV)

Today, almost twenty years since I first partook of the "Bread of Life," his love seems more real than ever. Daily I see ongoing evidence of it as he unfolds his plan for my life, which now includes my wife of eleven years and my four tremendous children. Yet it all began when I enthroned Jesus Christ as my Lord and Savior.

"But why does he leave the choice to me? Why doesn't he just force people to come under his Lordship?"

If I had the power of hypnotism and a little son, I could put him into a hypnotic state, thus robbing him of the power of intelligent choice. Then I could say, "Kiss me good night," and unfeeling arms would go around my neck, and unresponsive lips would be pressed to mine. I would have prompt and perfect obedience to my every command, but would I find satisfaction? No!

I want a son with a free will who is capable of disobeying me, but who willingly chooses to carry out my instructions, which are the outcome of my love for him and are given for his own good. I cannot conceive of God, who put these desires in my heart and yours, as being satisfied with anything less himself.

Jesus does not want puppets who jump in a given direction according to the wire that is pulled, nor does he want robots in the form of men who mechanically and absolutely obey his will as do the planets that whirl through space. The Bible tells us, "Love does not *demand* its own way" (1 Cor 13:5 TLB). And since God is love, he can find satisfaction in nothing less than the spontaneous love of our hearts and our freewill decisions to walk in paths that please and honor him. But it is obvious that this same power of free action enables us to defy and dishonor him if we so choose.

What about you? What choice have you made? What kingdom are you in? What path are you on?

The springboard for the rest of this book and the rest of your life is "Who's on your throne?"

If you have never turned to God from self, trusting Jesus to come into your life, forgive your sins (that means every sexual sin you've ever committed) and enable you to discover the fulfillment, purpose, and inner peace you desire, then will you be honest with him right now?

Jesus said if we want to follow him we must first "count the cost." It's not easy to do this, for we need to be willing to let go of any habit, any plan, any person, any activity that interferes with his marvelous design for our lives. We must commit ourselves to radical obedience of his Word—regardless of what our feelings or friends may dictate. Lordship means "an end to life on my own terms." To compromise or "sugar-coat" the cost is to "pervert the gospel" (Gal 1:7 RSV) and ultimately this deceives us from the truth. His call is not just to believe but to obey.

Yet if we'll look to Jesus not as a ho-hum, high, holy and unreachable marble god who's intent on making us miserable, but rather as our Creator and friend who's "for us and not against us" (Rom 8:31), the decision is obvious. Instead of being dragged to him kicking and screaming, we come willingly and fall into the security of his arms. Remember, Jesus loves us. He died on the cross to pay for our sins and wants to be our friend as well as our Lord—one who "sticks closer than a brother" (Prov 18:24 RSV). He's the "good shepherd" who sees us as sheep having gone astray. He wants to put us back on the path of life. Visualize him in this light.

Will you trust his love? Will you allow him to rescue (save) you from going in a way that ends in inevitable, spiritual death, in frustration, misery, and confusion? Will you acknowledge him as your Creator who paid the penalty for your sins, so you could be forgiven and reconciled to him?

If you are ready to yield yourself totally to Jesus, then speak these words to him:

"Jesus, thank you for loving me. Thank you for demonstrating that 'Greater love hath no man than this, that a man lay down his life for his friends' (John 15:13 KJV). Certainly you have shown your love for me. Right now I confess that I've been selfish—doing my own thing in the kingdom of darkness. But I now repent—turn around—and give you total control of my life. I declare an end to life in my own terms. I commit myself to obey the Word of God and let it be my standard throughout life. From this moment on I take my place in the kingdom of light and proudly proclaim Jesus Christ as Lord of my life."

If this prayer expresses the desire of your heart, pray it now. You become a new creation (2 Cor 5:17), enter a new kingdom, and launch out on a new path of life. Regardless of how dark and gloomy the future looks for the unrighteous of this world, you can move forward with quiet confidence undergirded by the promises of the Word of God.

> But the path of the righteous is like the light of dawn, which shines brighter and brighter until full day. (Prov 4:18 RSV)

TWO

God Wants a Generation of Radicals

REMEMBER YOUR BEST FRIEND GROWING UP? The one you shared, laughed, messed around and got in trouble with? The person with whom you made those crazy crank phone calls ("Oh, no—I hope he didn't recognize my voice!"), tried your first cigarette ("C'mon chicken—inhale it"), and launched out into that fascinating subject of sex ("Really! Where'd you hear that?").

Chuck was my best friend. We lived eight houses apart. We attended kindergarten, grade school, high school, and college together. We played with matches and later matched our wits. Twenty years of our young lives were spent in bonded friendship. There was no one with whom I was closer.

A few years ago my sister called long distance. She braced me by saying, "Larry." Then she blurted out, "Chuck is dead!"

"Huh?"

"His heart gave out; he's been on drugs, living with a girl, couldn't stop drinking. His dad's not even gonna have a funeral."

"But—but—what about his psychology degree—his future—he's only twenty-seven. . . ."

Replacing the receiver, I felt my legs start to buckle. Teardrops glazed my eyes as a lump blocked my swallow. Dropping to my knees, I anchored amidst the whirlwind.

"Satan has done it again!" I exploded, slamming my fist on our carpeted floor.

Holy hatred crackled and smoldered deep in the pit of my stomach as a Scripture verse flashed across my mind:

> The thief comes only in order that he may steal and may kill and may destroy. I came that they may have and enjoy life, and have it in abundance—to the full, till it overflows. (John 10:10 TAB)

John 10:10, more than any other verse in Scripture, conveys the intention of both Satan and Jesus for our lives. In my Bible I have the first part underlined in red and the second in green to ever remind me of the two separate plans.

Satan ("the thief") desires to rip us off—to "steal" away and "destroy" our future and, if possible, even to try to kill us.

Once, a fifty-year-old woman swiveled around and pointed her finger in my direction: "Larry, Satan hates your guts!"

Initially it hit me like a wet washrag in the face. But it's absolutely true. The sooner a realization of this sinks into our spirits the better off we'll be.

On the other hand, Jesus, our Good Shepherd, desires to lead us into an "abundant life." Instead of destructive plans for our future, his are totally constructive: "I know the plans I have for you . . . plans for welfare and not for evil, to give you a future and a hope" (Jer 29:11 RSV).

Most of us have a hard time believing what Jesus said. Satan, "the father of lies," works overtime to convince us that God is really a colossal spoilsport who delights in frustrating people, especially in matters of sex. After all, isn't that why the Bible was written—to inhibit us and prevent us from enjoying life?

For twenty years I believed this lie. I viewed God as a sinister, old gentleman—a celestial killjoy—peering over the portals of heaven, delighting in devising rigid rules intended to keep me in a straitjacket existence. To be a Christian meant to grit your teeth and sweat it out with an I-had-better-get-used-to-it type of attitude. After all, isn't this the impression that many derive from their religious upbringing?

Then one day I realized I was believing a bold-faced lie! It's a lie perpetuated by Satan to keep us in bondage to a belief that "God is against us." Embrace it and everything our Lord tells us to do becomes "one more thing to make us miserable."

If you've been believing this lie, it's time to crash through the fence and explode the myth! Smash it right now with sledge hammer force!

Jesus said that he came to give us abundant life. ("Abundant" in the Greek means "superabundant in quantity and superior in quality!")

His intention in giving us moral laws is not to inhibit or suppress us but rather to discipline us in a way that will catapult us into the realm of maximum fulfillment and the best life has to offer. When I view his commands as restrictions to my happiness rather than expressions of his love, I am siding with Satan, "the father of lies."

We're not serving some sour-faced ogre of a God.

We're not relegated to some ball-and-chain existence intended to warp our personality and stunt our creativity.

Jesus didn't save us to plop us down in the back pew of a church building, with our chins sagging to the floor, while we sing "Just As I Am" and remain "just as I was."

We serve a liberating Lord of whom the angels declared:

> Behold! I bring you *good news* of a *great joy* which will come to all the people. For to you is born this day in the town of David a Savior, Who is Christ, the Messiah, the Lord! (Luke 2:10 TAB)

We obey a smiling Savior who began his "Sermon on the Mount"—the distilled essence of his kingdom teaching—by telling us *nine* times the result of heeding his words: "Blessed are the . . . Blessed . . . Blessed . . ." (Greek, to be so full of joy as to be envied).

God wants a generation of radicals to be part of a "kingdom counterculture" emerging on the earth, reflecting "righteousness, peace, and joy" in a world of unrighteousness, confusion, and sorrow.

> The kingdom of God is not meat and drink; but righteousness, and peace, and joy in the Holy Ghost. (Rom 14:17 KJV)

What is the key to a kingdom lifestyle pulsating with life and overflowing with joy?

The answer is evident from the previous Scripture. *Righteousness* ("right living" according to his Word) leads to *peace* which then results in *joy*.

Said more simply, the key is: "Do right and you'll feel right!"

Some people gawk at and envy other radiant Christians and wonder "How?"

It's no mystery! *They obey the Word of God.*

It's a mistake to look for joyous living to come by some kind of benign magic or to expect it to come as a windfall apart from conditions known and met. There are plainly marked paths which lead straight to the green pastures. Let us walk in them.

Jesus enjoyed abundant life because he loved righteousness (right living) and hated lawlessness. "Thou hast loved righteousness and hated lawlessness; therefore God, thy God, hath anointed Thee with the *oil of gladness* above thy companions" (Heb 1:9 NAS).

We'll enjoy abundant life when we do the same—stay in "his presence" and at "his right hand" through obedience to his Word.

> Thou dost show me the path of life; In *thy* presence is fulness of joy, in *thy* right hand are pleasures for evermore! (Ps 16:11 RSV)

There is no other way.

Do right and you'll feel right.

For Christians who resist and disobey God's Word, there is guilt, sorrow, and depression. There is also a searching question from our Lord intended to get us back on the right "path."

> "Why do you call me 'Lord, Lord,' and not do what I tell you?" (Luke 6:46 RSV)

Since Satan knows our Lord's intention to bring forth a kingdom counterculture on the earth, his strategy is simple: keep us in darkness, ignorant of the Word of God. He knows that without it the people of God will be silenced in the face of worldly "foolosophies" and hence they will fail.

> My people are destroyed for lack of knowledge. (Hos 4:6 RSV)

Today, like never before, voices in the world are clamoring for our attention. The media—like a hydra-headed monster—are massaging and manipulating our minds at such an accelerated pace, many are totally unaware of what's happening.

The "prince of the power of the *air*" is seducing millions by his clever camouflage. Whether by television (our plug-in-drug), movies, radio, videos, magazines, or records, his insidious whisper can be detected, "anything goes—anything goes—anything goes—"

The result? Scripture is being fulfilled before our eyes.

> Every man did what was right in his own eyes. (Judg 21:25 RSV)

> Woe to those who call evil good and good evil; who put darkness for light and light for darkness, who put bitter for sweet and sweet for bitter! (Isa 5:20 RSV)

Arresting our attention in this hour is the voice of the Holy Spirit. Blowing an urgent trumpet throughout the land, he has a message for true followers of Jesus Christ: God wants a generation of radicals!

> Don't let the world around you squeeze you into its own mold, but let God remold your minds from within. (Rom 12:2 Phillips)

Radical end-time disciples are responding. With reckless abandonment and holy boldness we are publicly identifying ourselves with Jesus as part of an end-time kingdom counterculture. Daring to be different, refusing to compromise, motivated by a magnificent obsession, we hold our heads high and proudly proclaim:

> Though all the peoples walk / Each in the name of his god, / As for us, we will walk / In the name of the Lord our God forever and ever. (Mic 4:5 NAS)

Just as pagans cried out in the first century, so too will they once again say:

> These men who have turned the world upside down have come here also . . . saying that there is another king. (Acts 17:6-7 RSV)

King Jesus has declared that we, his kingdom counterculture, are not to wring our hands in despair but are to act as "salt" in preserving society from total corruption.

> You are the salt of the earth. (Matt 5:13 RSV)

People say, "Jesus is the light of the world." And this is true, but Jesus said, "As long as I am in the world, I am the light of the world" (John 9:5 RSV). Now that Jesus has ascended, the responsibility rests upon us. "You are the light of the world" (Matt 5:14 RSV).

In the midst of a decadent society where anything goes, we are part of the counter-offensive Jesus is launching against the avalanche of evil. Having the moral fiber and spiritual grit to stand against the tide, we bear witness to a collapsing world that there is another way of living, an alternate society, a kingdom counterculture "that cannot be shaken" (Heb 12:28). As Jesus said, we are to be "A city that is set on a hill [that] cannot be hid" (Matt 5:14 KJV).

We have made a quality decision—a determined setting of our will—that regardless of the abuse and persecution we may suffer, we are not following the crowd; we are following Christ! We're soldiers of the army he is raising up to save the world.

> By faith Moses, when he was grown up, refused to be called the son of Pharaoh's daughter, choosing rather to share ill-treatment with the people of God than to enjoy the fleeting pleasures of sin. He considered abuse suffered for the Christ greater wealth than the treasures of Egypt, for he looked to the reward. (Heb 11:24-26 RSV)

> Indeed all who desire to live a godly life in Christ Jesus will be persecuted. (2 Tim 3:12 RSV)

When persecuted, we respond in a way radically different from that of the world.

> Do not be overcome by evil, but overcome evil with good. (Rom 12:21 RSV)

> Love your enemies and pray for those who persecute you. (Matt 5:44 RSV)

The result? Because we unashamedly follow Christ, we are going to be unique—nonconformists—ordinary people living in an extraordinary way. We will be the "peculiar people" God intends us to be.

> But ye are a chosen generation, a royal priesthood, a holy nation, a peculiar people; that ye should shew forth the praises of him who hath called you out of darkness into his marvelous light: Which in time past were not a people, but are now the people of God. (1 Pet 2:9-10a KJV)

There can be no mistake that truly we are living in a different kingdom with different values, life styles, and relationships.

Kingdom of World	**Kingdom of God**
Satan—"The god of this world." (2 Cor: 4:4)	"Jesus Christ is Lord!" (Phil 2:11)
World Principles	**Biblical Principles**
1. Seeing is believing.	Believing is seeing (John 20:29).
2. Attain wisdom.	Become a fool (1 Cor 3:18).
3. Save your life.	Lose your life (Matt 16:25).
4. Be first.	Be last (Mark 9:35).

5. Achieve greatness.	Become least (Mark 10:43).
6. Be a leader.	Become a servant (Mark 10:43).
7. Exalt yourself.	Humble yourself (Luke 14:11).
8. Take the front seat.	Take a back seat (Luke 14:10).
9. Look out for your own interests.	Look out for the interests of others. Count others better than yourself (Phil 2:3).
10. Receive much.	Give much (Luke 6:38).
11. Make your good deeds known.	Keep your good deeds secret (Matt 6:3).
12. Love is a feeling and it is conditional.	Love is a lasting commitment and it is unconditional (1 Cor 13).
13. Love grows old.	Love never fails (1 Cor 13:8).
14. Hate your enemies.	Love your enemies (Matt 5:44)
15. Retaliate.	Forgive (Col 3:13).
16. Judge others.	Judge not (Matt 7:1).
17. Cover your mistakes.	Confess your mistakes (Prov 15:33).

18. Emphasize human might and human power.	It is "not by might, nor by power, but by my spirit" (Zech 4:6 KJV).
19. Eat, drink, and be merry, for tomorrow we die.	"Man shall not live by bread alone" (Matt 4:4 KJV).
20. Drown your sorrows.	"Be filled with the Spirit" (Eph 5:18 KJV).
21. It is impossible.	"All things are possible to him that believeth" (Mark 9:23 KJV).
22. Check your stars.	"Search the Scriptures" (John 5:39 KJV).
23. The Scripture was written by man.	"All scripture is given by inspiration of God" (2 Tim 3:16 KJV).
24. The Bible is outdated.	"Heaven and earth shall pass away but my words shall not pass away" (Matt 24:35 KJV).
25. Jesus was a good man.	Jesus is Lord! (Phil 2:11).
26. Jesus is dead.	"Jesus Christ the same yesterday, and today, and for ever!" (Heb 13:8 KJV).
27. Jesus is not coming again.	"I will come again, and receive you unto myself" (John 14:3 KJV).

28. I'll never worship Jesus Christ.	"Every knee should bow . . . and every tongue should confess that Jesus Christ is Lord!" (Phil 2:10, 11 KJV).

In the midst of dull, drab, humdrum humanity, each of us can take legitimate pride in our Christian uniqueness. We are radically different, having the courage to be distinctive. We shall stand out as men and women of God.

> Behold now, I perceive that this is a holy man of God. (2 Kings 4:9 KJV)

There is no area where our "radicalness" is more necessary than in the areas covered by this book. It takes real backbone to publicly identify with Jesus and his people by refusing to worship at the altar of illicit sex. To the carnal mind this teaching will appear as foolishness, but to genuine followers of Jesus Christ it will be a tree of life.

If you want to read popular opinion, you've got the wrong book. I'm not going to give it to you. God's way has never been popular. If you call yourself a disciple of Jesus Christ, you cannot heed the way the world does things. If you do, you disqualify yourself as his servant and take on the title of a "man pleaser."

> Am I now seeking the favor of men, or of God? Or am I trying to please men? If I were still pleasing men, I should not be a servant of Christ. (Gal 1:10 RSV)

All around us are a thousand and one voices, demonically inspired, trying to squeeze us into the world's mold. Will you excel above the mass of humanity and become one of the priceless few who have the courage to say "no?" It takes resurrection power to resist the world's "squeeze play"—

"If it feels good—do it."

"Do your own thing."

"Why wait til marriage?"

"Live together."

"Have an affair."

"Take the pill."

"Just get an abortion."

"Porno—what's the hassle?"

"Homosexual? Lesbian? Bisexual? Whatever turns you on."

"Everybody's doin' it."

"Just so it's meaningful."

"As long as nobody gets hurt."

"You've come a long way, baby."

"This is the new morality."

"Victorian days are over."

"C'mon outa the dark ages."

"C'mon outa the closet."

"Get rid of those hang-ups."

"Express yourself."

"Don't repress it."

"Go natural."

"Get with it."

"Be liberated."

"Be free."

"Let go."

"Live!"

"Be sure of this, that no immoral or impure man, or one who is covetous (that is, an idolater) has any inheritance in the kingdom of Christ and of God. *Let no one deceive you with empty words,* for it is because of these things that the wrath of God comes upon the sons of disobedience. . . . and try to learn what is pleasing to the Lord. Take no part in the unfruitful works of darkness, but instead expose them" (Eph 5:5-6,10-11 RSV).

"Claiming to be wise, they became fools. . . . Therefore God gave them up in the lusts of their hearts to impurity, to the dishonoring of their bodies among themselves, because they exchanged the truth about God for a lie and worshiped and served the creature rather than the Creator, who is blessed for ever! Amen.

"For this reason God gave them up to dishonorable passions. Their women exchanged natural relations for unnatural, and the men likewise gave up natural relations with women and were consumed with passion for one another, men committing shameful acts with men and receiving in their own persons the due penalty for their error. . . . Though they know God's decree that those who do such things deserve to die, they not only do them but approve those who practice them" (Rom 1:22-32 RSV).

"With their high-sounding nonsense they use the sensual pull of the lower passions to attract those who were just on the point of cutting loose from their companions in misconduct. They promise them liberty. Liberty!—when they themselves are bound hand and foot to utter depravity. For a man is the slave of whatever masters him" (2 Pet 2:18-19 Phillips).

We also hear those who say, "But what about all the ministers and religious people who say that a lot of these things are okay today because 'times have changed'? They say sexual relations before marriage are all right if they're 'meaningful'—petting is healthy so long as it's 'responsible'—homosexuality is normal—masturbation is a gift from God. They go to church buildings! They're *religious!*"

"Even Satan disguises himself as an angel of light. So it is not strange if his servants also disguise themselves as servants of righteousness. Their end will correspond to their deeds" (2 Cor 11:14-15 RSV).

"Preach the Word. . . . For the time is coming when people will not endure sound teaching, but having itching ears they will accumulate for themselves teachers to suit their own likings, and will turn away from listening to the truth and wander into myths" (2 Tim 4:2-4 RSV).

"But there were false prophets, too, in those days, just as there will be false teachers among you. They will cleverly tell their lies about God, turning against even their Master who bought them; but theirs will be a swift and terrible end. Many will follow their evil teaching that there is nothing wrong with sexual sin. And because of them Christ and His way will be scoffed at" (2 Pet 2:1-2 TLB).

When Jesus was asked about some of the signs of his return, he answered, "Take heed that no man deceive you" (Matt 24:4 KJV). God uses people to persuade you of his truth, and Satan uses people—even "religious" people—to deceive you. It is a war! It isn't a clean war; it is guerilla warfare on the part of Satan. You can't always tell who is the enemy.

"But understand this, that in the last days there will come times of stress. For men will be *lovers of self, lovers of money,* proud, arrogant, abusive, disobedient to their parents, ungrateful, unholy, inhuman, implacable, slanderers, profligates, fierce, haters of good, treacherous, reckless, swollen with conceit, *lovers of pleasure rather than lovers of God,* holding the form of religion but denying the power of it. Avoid such people" (2 Tim 3:1-5 RSV).

"But can the Bible really help us today? All these modern, sophisticated sex practices that are going on—how can the Bible guide us when they're all so new?"

"There is nothing new under the sun. Is there anything of which one might say 'See this, it is new'? Already it has existed for ages which were before us" (Eccles 1:9-10 NIV).

Let's check out just how "ahead of its time" the Word of God really is concerning so-called "new" and "modern" sex practices:

1. *Make Out (petting)*—"It is right for a man not to touch (Greek, "light the fires" of passion in) a woman" (1 Cor 7:1 KJV).

2. *Have Sex/Live Together (fornication)*—"For this is the will of God . . . that you abstain from immorality. . . . whoever disregards this, disregards not man but God, who gives his Holy Spirit to you" (1 Thess 4:3, 8 RSV).

3. *Have an Affair/Open Marriage (adultery)*—"Let marriage be held in honor among all, and let the marriage bed be undefiled; for God will judge the immoral and adulterous" (Heb 13:4 RSV).

4. *Be Gay/Come Out of the Closet (homosexuality and lesbianism)*—"Do not be deceived; neither the immoral, nor idolators, nor adulterers, nor homosexuals . . . will inherit the kingdom of God" (1 Cor 6:9-10 RSV).

5. *Try Bisexuality*—"You shall not lie with a male as with a woman; it is an abomination" (Lev 18:22 RSV).

6. *What's wrong with being a hooker if you want to? (prostitution)*—"Do you not know that he who joins himself to a prostitute becomes one body with her? . . . Shun immorality" (1 Cor 6:16, 18 RSV).

7. *Enjoy pornography. There's nothing wrong with nudity*—"You shall not uncover the nakedness of a woman and of her daughter" (Lev 18:17 RSV).

8. *Be a transvestite*—"A woman shall not wear anything that pertains to a man, nor shall a man put on a woman's garment; for whoever does these things is an abomination to the Lord your God" (Deut 22:5 RSV).

9. *Try Bestiality*—"You shall not lie with any beast and defile yourself with it, neither shall any woman give herself to a beast to lie with it: it is perversion" (Lev 18:23 RSV).

10. *Fantasizing turns you on. Go ahead.*—"But she carried her harlotry further; she saw men portrayed upon the wall, the images of the Chaldeans portrayed in vermilion . . . When she saw them she doted [Hebrew, lusted or "breathed sensually"] upon them, and sent messengers to them in Chaldea. And the Babylonians came to her into the bed of love, and they defiled her with their lust; and after she was polluted by them, she turned from them in disgust" (Ezek 23:14, 16-17 RSV).

11. *Buy some modern sex devices for yourself*—"You also took your fair jewels of my gold and of my silver, which I had given you, and made for yourself images of men, and with them played the harlot" (Ezek 16:17 RSV).

12. *Be sensual. Seduce a man*—"Now Joseph was handsome and good-looking. And after a time his master's wife cast her eyes upon Joseph and said, 'Lie

with me.' but he refused. . . . But one day, when he went into the house to do his work and none of the men of the house was there in the house, she caught him by his garment, saying, 'Lie with me.' But he left his garment in her hand, and fled and got out of the house" (Gen 39:6b-8, 11-12 RSV).

13. *How about incest? It's a new way to turn on!* "It is actually reported that there is immorality among you, and of a kind that is not found even among pagans; for a man is living with his father's wife. . . . Let him who has done this be removed from among you" (1 Cor 5:1-2 RSV).

14. *Hear the latest seducing techniques?*—"I have perfumed my bed with myrrh, aloes, and cinnamon. Come, let us take our fill of love till morning. . . . With much seductive speech she persuades him; with her smooth talk she compels him. All at once he follows her, as an ox goes to the slaughter . . . he does not know that it will cost him his life" (Prov 7:17, 18, 21-23 RSV).

15. *Let's party! Booze and sex is where it's at*—"Come, let us make our father drink wine, and we will lie with him. . . . So they made their father drink wine that night; and the first-born went in, and lay with her father" (Gen 19:32-33 RSV).

16. *Dabble in the occult to find out what the future holds*—"There shall not be found among you anyone who . . . uses divination, one who practices witchcraft, or one who interprets omens (astrologer), or a sorcerer, or one who casts a spell (hypnotist), or a medium, or a spiritist, or one who calls up the dead. For whoever does these things is detestable to the Lord" (Deut 18:10-12 NAS).

17. *But there are a lot of religious leaders who say this stuff*

is okay—"But I have this against you, that you tolerate the woman Jezebel, who calls herself a prophetess and is teaching and beguiling my servants to practice immorality.... I gave her time to repent, but she refuses to repent of her immorality" (Rev 2:20-21 RSV).

But why is God against sex?

He's not! He's not against the *use* of sex, only its *abuse*. He is totally *for* sex in marriage; totally *against* it outside of marriage. How can anyone think God doesn't like sex when he thought it up in the first place?

God created all parts of the human body. He did not create some parts good and some bad; He created them all good, for when he had finished his creation, he looked at it and said, "It is all very good" (Gen 1:31).

Let's consider just two accounts in Scripture that should explode for all time the misconception that God is the world's biggest "wet blanket."

"Your breasts are as two fawns, twins of a gazelle.... You have ravished my heart, my sister, my bride.... Your lips drop honey, my bride, honey and milk are under your tongue. Your rounded thighs are a jeweled chain. ... Your navel is as a rounded bowl in which mingled wine is never lacking; your belly as a heap of wheat, set about with lilies. How beautiful you are, my love ... your breasts are as clusters of grapes ... I will climb into my palm tree, I will take hold of the branches of it. Your breasts shall be as clusters of vines, the fragrance of your breath as of apples. The roof of your mouth is like red wine" (Song of Sol 4:5, 9, 11; 7:1-9 Berkeley).

"Rejoice with the wife of your youth. . . . Let her breasts satisfy thee at all times; and be thou ravished (intoxicated) always with her love" (Prov 5:18, 19 KJV).

Our Lord celebrates the sensual. After all, he made all things for us "richly to enjoy" (1 Tim 6:17). Yet he also says, "I adjure you . . . that you stir not up nor awaken love until it please" (Song of Sol 8:4 RSV).

There's the key.

The Bible always speaks approvingly of a sexual relationship—as long as it is confined to married partners. The only prohibition on sex in the Word of God relates to premarital or extramarital activity. Without question, the Bible is absolutely clear on that subject, condemning all such conduct. *Therefore, all sexual activity outside the bonds of marriage is sin and that will never change.*

End-time disciples of Jesus Christ know that we are part of a kingdom counterculture that God is raising up on the earth. We are a people with courage to say "no" to any kind of physical intimacy outside of the will of God. We want to please our Lord who loved us and gave himself for us. We want to walk in "abundant life," refusing to give "any opportunity to the devil" (Eph 4:27). Also, we want to experience the maximum marriage that he intends for us.

Ecclesiastes, chapter three, probably conveys the best conviction Jesus has implanted in our hearts:

> For everything there is a season, and a time for every matter under heaven . . . a time to embrace, and a time to refrain from embracing . . . . He has made everything beautiful in its time. (Eccles 3:1, 5b, 11 RSV)

THREE

Our Heart's Desires

"DOES IT *REALLY* WORK? I mean, if I follow God's plan for love, sex and marriage can I be certain that it'll bring success? He won't give me a raw deal or stick me with a lemon, will he?"

Whenever teaching goes forth on this subject matter, questions such as the above are inevitable. (I know—I had them all the time.) They're legitimate. They're honest. They deserve a response.

Scripturally this is easy. For those who obey God's Word and are not willing to settle for less than God's best, consider:

"Trust in the Lord, and do good; so you will dwell in the land, and enjoy security. Take delight in the Lord, and he will give you the desires of your heart. Commit your way to the Lord; trust in him, and he will act" (Ps 37:3-5 RSV).

"Seek first his kingdom and his righteousness, and all these things shall be yours as well" (Matt 6:33 RSV).

"If you then, who are evil, know how to give good gifts to your children, how much more will your Father who is in heaven give good things to those who ask him!" (Matt 7:11 RSV).

"No good thing does the Lord withhold from those who walk uprightly" (Ps 84:11 RSV).

Then there's the classic—

> Trust in the Lord with all your heart, and lean not upon your own understanding. In all your ways acknowledge him, and he shall direct your paths. (Prov 3:5-6)

Besides the Word there is also the Word made flesh.

Rather than preaching a sermon, let me share with you from my experience—as one who struggled with sexual temptation, battled raunchy thoughts, confessed regretful "slips," and fought off condemnation.

When the day finally arrived to walk up that aisle and meet the woman destined to be my wife, we could both say—beyond the shadow of a doubt—it really does work!

On April 10, 1976, over 1,200 people assembled to witness the glorious event....

"A covenant is a solemn agreement between two parties," the message began. "It is the oldest rite that is known to man."

What followed was a clear and concise unfolding of the ancient rite of entering covenant. My friend Paul cited the "removal of coats" as symbolic of one's resources becoming the other's; "removal of belts" conveying strength available when needed; "killing an animal" suggesting death to one's independence; "cutting one's flesh and mingling of blood" symbolic that the parties were now in covenant; and "changing of names" plus "celebration of covenant meal" to seal the covenant in the eyes of all.

He then proceeded to apply these insights to our covenant marriage celebration.

"Although there is no formal coat or belt removal," he said, "both Larry and Doris know their resources and strengths now become one—their savings, possessions, even the VWs! In place of a slain animal is their verbal commitment today of death to their independence and personal 'rights.'

"Cutting covenant and the resultant mark is seen in the exchange of rings. Henceforth, wherever they go, observers will see the ring as the permanent mark of ones who are in covenant. The name change is obvious as Doris Grefenstette becomes Doris Tomczak. And the covenant meal will take place in a few minutes as they 'cut' the cake and place a piece in each other's mouths. This is not a silly gesture devoid of meaning, but a public declaration—'all I have now becomes part of you.' "

The oft-quoted definition of agape love—the one hanging on my bedroom door for years—suddenly flashed in my mind. "Agape love is a costly act of the will for the greatest good of the other person."

When the moment arrived for the exchange of vows, Doris and I knelt, clasped hands, and rested in what seemed to be a spiritual bubble of intimacy. Enabled by his Spirit, we gently inscribed these vows on one another's hearts.

"Doris, the Word of God teaches, 'Husbands, love your wives as Christ loved the church and gave himself up for her that he might sanctify her by the washing of water through the Word,' so I now vow to love you just like Jesus loved the church. I'll give myself up for you, in order to sanctify or set you apart for the abundant life that Jesus designed for you.

"The Word says, 'Husbands should love their wives as their own bodies and nourish and cherish them,' I now vow before God to love you as I love my own body and that I'll cherish you. In other words, I'll affectionately care for you. I'll nourish you, protect and provide for you. I make that a permanent binding vow.

"Scripture says, 'Husbands should dwell with their wives in knowledge'—knowing my leadership responsibilities and knowing your unique needs as a woman. It says I should 'honor you as the weaker vessel.' I vow to do just that by the power of his Holy Spirit. I will honor—treat you as precious—and minister to you, aware of your feminine needs.

"The Bible says, 'Husbands should give their wives their marital rights.' I vow today that I will never refuse you sexually, but meet your needs always.

"The Bible also teaches that we're to 'speak the truth in love to each other.' Today I vow, by God's grace, that I'll never tell you a lie—never.

"It also commands, 'Never let the sun go down on your anger,' so I vow never to allow this to happen. When we have misunderstandings, I will take the initiative to see to it that they are cleared up before bed.

"Finally, God's Word says, 'What God has joined together, let no man put asunder.' This day I vow that in our marriage, divorce is not even an option. This union is permanent from this day forward.

"These are the scriptural vows I make to you today, Doris. These are the Word of God, and by the grace of

God, I'll fulfill them in our lives, in the name of our Lord Jesus."

I allowed a smile to surface as I leaned forward to hear the words of my soon-to-be wife.

Her eyes glistening, Doris began.

"Larry, I don't have any doubt that it's God's will for us to be married. I know that he ordained that we should become one. Because I know it's his will and because I love you, I want to make these vows to you in the name of our Lord Jesus.

"The Word of God teaches that 'a married woman is concerned about worldly affairs and how she can please her husband.' By his grace, I'll spend the rest of my life trying to please you and meet your needs.

"God's Word teaches that 'a woman is bound to her husband as long as he lives,' so by God's grace and the power of His Holy Spirit, I'll gladly live with you as your wife until the Lord takes us home.

"Larry, the Word teaches that 'the head of every man is Christ and the head of the woman is her husband.' So by God's grace and the power of His Spirit from now on I'll look to you for my leadership. I'll submit to your decisions. I'll obey your will in everything as I would the Lord Jesus himself. I'll respect you, admire you, and reverence you, and I'll teach our children to do the same.

"And Larry, the Word teaches that 'you're to rejoice in the wife of your youth' and that 'my affections are to fill you with delight at all times.' So by his grace and the power of His Holy Spirit I'll keep you always intoxicated with my love.

"I love you."

Within what appeared to be seconds, our celebrant

said, "I now pronounce you man and wife!" The moment he did, I vividly recall an actual "thud" on the inside. That's the only way I can describe it. I actually sensed a soft explosion deep in the core of my being as we became "one flesh" in the eyes of God.

The rest of the service? Well, let's just say it progressed with glorious smoothness and swiftness.

And then . . . Doris and I were pillowing our heads, embraced in each other's arms.

"Stir not up nor awaken love until it please" (Song of Sol 2:7 RSV).

The bedroom in which we fell asleep that night is similar to the one which we share today. On our walls hangs a parchment. On it are written, word for word, our wedding vows. They're there for a purpose: for reflection, review and response. I find myself going there often.

Our life together, even when misunderstandings arise (and they do!), is becoming a fulfillment of the Scripture we placed on the cover of our wedding invitations:

"And you shall write my words upon the doorposts of your house and upon your gates, that your days and the days of your children may be multiplied in the land . . . as the days of heaven upon the earth" (Deut 11:20-21).

"Heaven on earth?!"

Yes, that's what our loving heavenly Father intends.

Sow obedience—reap the benefits.

Sow disobedience—reap the consequences.

Which one will you choose?

It really does work!

FOUR

Why Wait Til Marriage?

"YOU'VE GOTTA DO whatever makes you *feel* good!"
Ever hear that line before?

Anyone who's been around the past few years (and is not under Christ's Lordship) has probably not only heard it but, chances are, they've bought it.

"Is it *right?*"

Consider:

There are only two ways of life. One says: "I shall live according to *feeling*"; the other: "I shall live according to what God *says.*" The first is based on selfishness; the second on the Word of God. These two life styles are diametrically opposed to each other and, depending on which one you choose, they determine your destiny in life.

As stated earlier, a person living according to feeling is in the kingdom of self and his motto is "*My* will be done." Instead of *thy* kingdom come and *thy* will be done" he says, "*My* kingdom come and the sooner the better!"

Today there's a lot of talk about "being free"—liberated to do as you feel. Sex before marriage, living together, having an affair, getting an abortion, choosing a "gay" lifestyle, etc., are all "valid ways to express your freedom and do as you feel." After all, it's the "new morality" and "who's to say what's wrong or right?" If anyone objects, the argument follows, "Times have changed. Everybody's doin' it—therefore it must be okay."

Is this right?

As radical, end-time disciples of Jesus Christ, our response is a resounding "no." We will not compromise our Christian principles in this day of permissiveness. We absolutely refuse to bend with the times and jump on a bandwagon headed for disaster. God has established standards in his Word and we mean business about carrying them out.

The "everybody's doin' it" argument is not only false but it is the most deadly, insidious doctrine being promoted today. It's a cleverly frosted deception of Satan to bring millions of people into bondage and ultimately shatter their lives. Christ came into our lives to set us free from that sort of social pressure. Christians live their lives on the basis of biblical conviction, not social consensus.

"What about the statement, 'Times have changed'?"

They may have but God hasn't and neither have the timeless principles of his Word. Our Lord isn't old-fashioned and neither is he modern. Scripture says:

> Jesus Christ is the *same* yesterday and today and for ever. (Heb 13:8 RSV)

"Who's to say what's right or wrong?"

If Jesus had meant for us to live in a world of moral

uncertainty he would have given us ten suggestions rather than ten *commandments.*

In this "new morality" we're told to "be free—shed your hang-ups—do what feels good—express your innermost feelings" regardless of what they might be. Anger, lust, hate—let them out. Be honest. Satisfy those inner cravings. You have a duty to them, for therein lies "the real you."

So a woman encountering marital problems heeds the advice of a therapist: "What you need to put life back into your marriage is an affair. It'll give you more confidence in yourself and bring a new freshness into your marriage." So, she follows his advice. Reluctantly. Does it heal her marriage? Of course not. On top of her initial dissatisfaction, she now has to cope with unfaithfulness, guilt, deceit, fears, and her marriage completely falls apart.

"I am anxious for you with the deep concern of God himself—anxious that your love should be for Christ alone, just as *a pure maiden saves her love for one man only, for the one who will be her husband"* (2 Cor 11:2 TLB).

Two young people go partying and discover themselves powerfully drawn to one another. He views her with X-ray eyes and thinks, "I feel horny. That foxy babe looks all right."

She feels real sexy and thinks, "He's sure good-lookin.'" Later they find themselves parked in a secluded spot—both get hot-and-heavy—there's a momentary thrill—then it's over. He quickly drops her off, yet she can't help feeling "used," discarded like a piece of Kleenex. He drives home with the music extra loud, glad he's got someone else lined up for tomorrow.

"Then Amnon (after he had laid with her) hated her with very great hatred; so that the hatred with which he hated her was greater than the love with which he had loved her. And Amnon said to her, 'Arise, be gone'" (2 Sam 13:15 RSV).

"Free sex?"

Yes, free to be sexually active, but not free to escape the consequences.

"New morality?"

No, simply the old immorality put in new terms.

Only Christians can experience true freedom. Not freedom to obey the impulses of our lower nature like animals, but freedom to choose obedience to the Word of God. Biblical freedom is not the ability to do as I want; it's the power to do as I ought. That's why Jesus came.

> If you continue in my word, you are truly my disciples, and you will know the truth, and the truth will make you free. . . . So if the Son makes you free, you will be free indeed. (John 8:31, 36 RSV)

What's the evidence of this freedom?

Instead of being enslaved to selfishness (demanding what I feel and what I want), one is free to serve others from a heart of love.

> For you were called to freedom, brethren; only do not use your freedom as an opportunity for the flesh, but through love be servants of one another. (Gal 5:13 RSV)

How liberating! Instead of being trapped in a prison of selfishness, we're free to be genuinely concerned for the welfare of others. This is the kingdom counter-culture emerging on the earth!

Unbelievers know nothing about this freedom. They think they're free but actually they're enslaved to sin.

Take, for instance, the atheistic father of modern psychiatry—Sigmund Freud. He pioneered much of what we hear today: "Let go of inhibitions. Stop repressing your sex drives. Be a free spirit. Let yourself go."

On September 21, 1939, Sigmund Freud took the hand of the physician at his bedside and said, "My dear Schur, you promised not to forsake me when my time comes. Now it is nothing but torture and makes no sense any more."

Of what was he dying?

Years before, Sigmund's doctor listened to his irregular heartbeat and suggested he stop his heavy cigar smoking. Dr. Freud stopped for a short time, but became so miserable that he resumed the habit.

He suffered through thirty-five operations for cancer of the jaw, finally losing his entire lower jaw. Physicians warned him repeatedly that he was risking his life by continuing to smoke. But the tobacco habit had him enslaved and he finally died of cancer.

Dr. Freud could analyze the human mind apart from God. He could identify his problem. But by himself he could not conquer himself.

As Christians we've been set free. We have the ability to sin but no longer the obligation. Instead of "If it feels good do it," we proclaim:

To obey is better than sacrifice. (1 Sam 15:22 RSV)

It may be hard at times—even Jesus "learned obedience through what He suffered" (Heb 5:8 RSV)—yet we know: The will of God will never lead me where the grace of God cannot sustain me. "I can do all things through Christ which strengtheneth me" (Phil 4:13 KJV).

"What's so wrong with two people sleeping together or even living together if they really love each other, and are open and honest?"

"Not with just anybody—but what if it's a *meaningful* relationship?"

"What if we have sex, enjoy it, and discover it makes us love each other all the more?"

All right. Let's tackle it—straightforwardly.

First, "to write the same things to you is not irksome to me, and is safe for you" (Phil 3:1 RSV).

Jesus came not as a divine wet blanket to spoil our enjoyment of life, but he came as one who loves us and desires for us to "have and enjoy life, and have it in abundance—to the full, till it overflows" (John 10:10 TAB).

The only way to consistently abide (dwell) in "abundant life" is through uncompromising obedience to what he commands (not suggests) us to do. There simply is no other way.

"As the Father has loved me, so have I loved you; abide in my love. If you keep my commandments, you will abide in my love, just as I have kept my Father's commandments and abide in his love. These things I have spoken to you, that my joy may be in you, and that your joy may be full" (John 15:9-11 RSV).

In other words, Jesus gives us moral laws not to undercut our enjoyment of life and frustrate us like muzzled hounds at a barbecue, but he gives them because *he loves us and desires to discipline us in a way that will best bring us into the fullness of all life has to offer.* The key is knowing the person behind these laws—that he loves us and demonstrated it on Calvary. Otherwise they appear as just some legalistic code.

In the area of sex, God has put limitations on the display of physical affection prior to marriage because he wants us to experience a maximum marriage with a maximum sex life.

"But why do we have to follow rules and regulations? Why can't we be 'free' to do what we want to do?"

Laws are essential in every area of life in order to maintain order and harmony. In the area of our *physical body* there are many rules. We human beings must eat food and drink water, or we'll die. Eat too much with the thought, "Who needs rules?" and we'll balloon up and become a cathedral instead of a temple.

In the *mental and emotional realms* one must follow rules and regulations to become stable and mature. A person who is self-centered, increasingly fearful of people, distrusts himself and lives in isolated anxiety ends up unable to cope with life or himself.

In *sports,* there's always a book of rules. Imagine the mess if everyone decided to "do their thing" in a baseball game—the batter steps up holding a cucumber instead of a bat; the pitcher stands on first base and throws watermelons; five guys huddle together in right field holding hockey sticks, etc.

In *society* we have laws against stealing, murder, adultery. Without them we'd degenerate into anarchy, a "dog-eat-dog" jungle. Wherever we turn in life we are confronted by laws—rules and regulations. The key is to see them as our friends and not our enemies.

And what are God's regulations for human sexuality?

Straightforward: *God explicitly condemns all forms of premarital sex.* Petting, fondling, stroking, touching, caressing the more intimate parts of another's body—either through the clothing or by direct contact—is forbidden outside the bonds of marriage. It is sin. It will never change.

"Whew! Isn't it good to have it straight-from-the-shoulder and know what God's standards are for us, his children?" Remember what I said before: To the world this will appear as foolishness, but to genuine disciples of Jesus Christ it will be life and health.

God's plan is chastity (purity) before marriage and fidelity (loyalty) after marriage.

Chastity is not a negative principle. It does not refer to the repressing of legitimate, natural desires, nor their denial. It is keeping sex in the *right place* for the *right person* at the *right time.* It means sex controlled, not controlling.

"But what if I've already blown it? What if I've fallen into immorality—already committed fornication—had an abortion . . . ?"

If you're guilty of sexual sin *before* you yielded your life to the Lordship of Jesus Christ, relax and rejoice in your spirit that now you are a totally "new creation (Greek, a new species of being that never existed before), the old has passed away, behold, the new has come!" (2 Cor 5:17 RSV). This is the miracle of the new birth: *Even a prostitute becomes pure when she yields her life to Christ.*

"What if I'm pregnant with an illegitimate child right

now and every kick of the baby brings guilt and condemnation?"

If you've repented and confessed your sin then shout, "There is therefore now *no* condemnation for those who are in Christ Jesus" (Rom 8:1 RSV) and let every kick bring you a reminder of the love, mercy and total forgiveness of a God who "remembers our sins no more" (Heb 10:17). Think with each movement, "I've forgiven you. I love you. I've forgiven you. . . ." Claim his promise that he will "give to them beauty for ashes, the oil of joy for mourning, the garment of praise for the spirit of heaviness" (Isa 61:3).

If you're guilty of sexual sin *after* yielding your life to his Lordship, confess your sin to God. Repent (turn around) and forsake your sin to serve him who loves you. "He who conceals his transgressions will not prosper, but he who confesses and forsakes them will obtain mercy" (Prov 28:13 RSV).

If your actions have harmed others, often it is good to confess the wrong (without projecting guilt on them) saying, "The Lord has shown me that *I* was wrong and I'd like to ask you to forgive me."

Don't forget to forgive yourself and trust your loving, heavenly Father to use even your mistakes for good (Rom 8:28). Stand strong in the assurance that God has forgiven and forgotten your sins and now will empower you to live a life that is a credit to his name. (When Satan, "the accuser of the brethren day and night," comes to grab a "guilt handle" and remind you of your past, have the following Scriptures handy in your heart or on a piece of paper to "quench all his fiery darts": 1 John 1:9, Ps 103:12, Mic 7:19, Isa 1:18, Jer 31:34, Matt 18:21-22.)

Now let's spell it out a little more clearly:

Why wait till marriage?

1. God commands it.
2. We'll reap what we sow in the present.
3. We'll reap what we sow in the future.

God Commands It

Let's stop spending hours wading through books and magazines by so-called "Christian authorities" who are trying to legitimize sinful behavior, compromise the Word of God and genuflect to the devil. I know; I've read scores of books and magazines full of these damnable heresies which are sheer poison to readers: "The Bible is vague in this area. Certainly there are forms of 'responsible petting' which are healthy." "Nowhere does the Bible really state clearly that sexual experimentation outside of marriage is wrong." "Masturbation is actually a gift of God." "Not all homosexuality is wrong." "Scripture seems to be silent on many of these questions." This kind of spiritual gobbledegook grieves my spirit and, at the same time, it makes my blood boil. It is exactly what God used to jolt me into writing this book!

Knowing that "we who teach shall be judged with greater strictness" (James 3:1 RSV), and we must "learn not to go beyond that which is written" (1 Cor 4:6 TAB), I prefer to let God's Word speak for itself.

"My son, beware of anything beyond these (words). Of making many books there is no end, and much study is a weariness of the flesh. The end of the matter; all has been heard. Fear God, and keep his commandments; for this is the whole duty of man" (Eccles 12:12-13 RSV).

And what are his commandments on premarital sex? Let's see how vague and silent he really is.

> Let marriage be held in honor among all, and the marriage bed be undefiled; for God will judge the immoral and adulterous. (Heb 13:4 RSV)

Notice the four points:

1. *Marriage is an honorable institution*—something God ordained as sacred. It's not to be ridiculed ("Hear the one about the divorcee" or "Who needs marriage? Just live together") or treated lightly ("We'll get married, try it and if it doesn't work—").

2. *The marriage bed is to be undefiled* ("chastity should be respected by you all"—Phillips)—the marriage bed is reserved as a place of enjoyment and total communication between a husband and wife and must never be contaminated by deviation from God's plan.

3. *God will bring judgment upon the immoral* (Some translations say "fornicators." The Greek word means more than sexual relations between unmarrieds. It is an inclusive word which may also include adultery, incest, homosexuality and other kinds of sex sin. See 1 Corinthians 5:1 and Jude 7.)—judgment befalls those violating God's moral laws in any way.

4. *God will bring judgment upon the adulterous*—adultery refers to persons engaging in sexual relations with someone other than their spouses. In other words, those who break the laws of God shall themselves be broken.

> "Have you not read that he who made them from the beginning made them male and female, and said, 'For

> this reason a man shall leave his father and mother and be joined to his wife and the two shall become one flesh'? So they are no longer two but one flesh. What therefore God has joined together, let no man put asunder." (Matt 19:4-6 RSV)

Notice the sequence: 1. leave 2. cleave 3. become one flesh. ("Cleave" means "to glue together." Cleaving is meant to be *permanent.*) For those deceived individuals who say God is opposed to casual, promiscuous sexual relations but does not forbid sex relations between couples "really in love," examine the sequence cited by Jesus.

First, "leave"—a movement away from one family in order to enter another. Second, "cleave"—the two are joined (glued) permanently together. Third, "become one flesh"—the couple *now* has the privilege of consummating their marriage in sexual relations. God does not permit us to invert his divine order to take the privileges without the responsibilities.

> "Flee immorality." (1 Cor 6:18 NAS)
> "Avoid sexual looseness like the plague." (1 Cor 6:18 Phillips)
> "Run from sex sin." (1 Cor 6:18 TLB)

An excellent illustration of this principle is the story of young Joseph fleeing from Potiphar's wife after her attempted seduction (Gen 39:6-23). "She caught him by his garment, saying, 'Lie with me.' But he left his garment in her hand, and fled and got out of the house" (v 12).

Do you not know that the unrighteous will not inherit the kingdom of God? Do not be deceived; neither the immoral, nor idolators, nor adulterers, nor sexual perverts, nor thieves, nor the greedy, nor drunkards, nor revilers, nor robbers will inherit the kingdom of God. And such were some of you. But you were washed, you were sanctified, you were justified in the name of the Lord Jesus Christ and in the Spirit of our God.

"All things are lawful for me," but not all things are helpful. "All things are lawful for me," but I will not be enslaved by anything. "Food is meant for the stomach and the stomach for food"—and God will destroy both one and the other. The body is not meant for immorality, but for the Lord, and the Lord for the body. And God raised the Lord and will also raise us up by his power. Do you not know that your bodies are members of Christ? Shall I therefore take the members of Christ and make them members of a prostitute? Never! Do you not know that he who joins himself to a prostitute becomes one body with her? For, as it is written, "The two shall become one flesh." But he who is united to the Lord becomes one spirit with him. Shun immorality. Every other sin which a man commits is outside the body; but the immoral man sins against his own body. Do you not know that your body is a temple of the Holy Spirit within you, which you have from God? You are not your own; you were bought with a price. So glorify God in your body. (1 Cor 6:9-20 RSV)

Notice especially verses nine and ten. Also notice that

the next verse says, "And such *were* some of you. But you were washed, you were sanctified, you were justified in the name of the Lord Jesus." In other words, here God clearly condemns homosexuality and at the same time explicitly proclaims liberation from it. Proof is seen in the fact that some in Corinth were once homosexual but they had been set free! (So much for the argument, "Once a homosexual, always a homosexual.")

Also, notice verse 16, "Do you not know that he who joins himself to a prostitute becomes one body with her? For as it is written, 'The two shall become one flesh.' " For people who cheapen sex by a casual approach (i.e., "It's no big deal"—"Do it"—"I'm on the lookout for a lay"), God says that even if you go to bed with a prostitute, you are still "one flesh" with her—that is, powerfully and spiritually tied together.

Sexual intercourse is far more than just a physical act—more than two unclad, perspiring bodies grappling together under the bed covers. You know that if you walk into a room and see a person you've slept with, there's just something indefinable there. Sex is a *total* trip, and because of the totality of the act, it demands total commitment in marriage. The other person has to be willing to say, "I'm yours for life." To give yourself sexually for anything less than that is a sellout and it is rooted in total *self*ishness. ("*I* think we should just live together so *I* can use you when *I* want. After all, *I* may get tired of you and *I* may want out. *I* gotta be sure you don't hinder *me* from doing *my* thing.")

Here's one of the most comprehensive passages in the New Testament on the use and abuse of sex.

> You will remember the instructions we gave you then in the name of the Lord Jesus. God's plan is to make you holy, and that entails first of all a clean cut with sexual immorality. Every one of you should learn to control his body, keeping it pure and treating it with respect. (1 Thess 4:2-4 Phillips)

"A clean cut with sexual immorality"—no exceptions, no "but if they're in love" or "maybe if the couple is engaged."

"Learn to control his body"—a fire is warm and wonderful in the fireplace under control; but if that same fire is set loose it can also burn down the house. Water is refreshing in the tap under control; but that same water rushing through a broken dam on a rampage can devastate an area and destroy human life. The difference? *Control.*

The sex drive is a tremendous, dynamic power that God has implanted within us. Under control, it works for us, blesses us, enriches our existence. The key is controlling it in the overcoming power of Jesus the way he instructs us in his Word. Out of control, it can ruin our lives, bring untold heartache and misery.

> That no man transgress and *defraud* his brother in the matter, because the Lord is the avenger in all these things, just as we . . . solemnly warned you. (1 Thess 4:6 NAS)

Defraud means "arousing sexual desires in another person that cannot be *righteously* satisfied." It means turning someone else on sexually when you know you can't go through with it.

Why don't you read that again. It is extremely important.

Here's how it applies:

Satan has deceived many couples into believing that there is a way to "go all the way" without "going all the way." Some call it "everything but." That is, they engage in extremely intimate sex play ("petting"), yet stop short of sexual union. Petting behavior may include (either directly or through the clothing) fondling of the girl's breasts, touching and rubbing one another's genitals (or in the general vicinity), possibly placing bare genitals together but avoiding penetration, etc. The rationalization is, "This isn't wrong because we're not 'going all the way.' We're just expressing our love for one another."

Do you know what rationalization is? Someone defines it: "Looking for reasons in our mind to justify that which we know in our spirit to be wrong."

"But we can always stop. We've got things under control."

NOTE: "Let any one who thinks that he stands take heed lest he fall" (1 Cor 10:12 RSV).

Once again, let me say it straightforwardly: God *explicitly condemns all forms of premarital sex.* Petting, fondling, stroking, touching, caressing the more intimate parts of another's body—either through the clothing or by direct contact—is forbidden outside the bonds of marriage. It is sin. It will never change.

Now petting is not wrong. It isn't sinful or dirty, that is, in its right place. Petting is the God-given means of bringing a husband and wife into the sexual act. But out of place it is sinful and can bring frustration, disillusionment, heartache and contempt. That is why our Lord speaks so clearly about its misuse.

> That no man transgress and defraud his brother (or sister) in the matter. (1 Thess 4:6 NAS)
>
> It is good for a man not to touch a woman. (The Greek word for "touch" means "to kindle, set on fire the passions.") (1 Cor 7:1 KJV)
>
> ". . . And it was I (the Lord) who kept you from sinning against me; therefore I did not let you touch her." (Gen 20:6 RSV)
>
> Can a man carry fire in his bosom and his clothes not be burned? Or can one walk upon hot coals and his feet not be scorched? (Prov 6:27-28 RSV)
>
> Treat younger women like sisters, in all purity. (1 Tim 5:2 RSV) (Phillips version says, "like sisters, ***and nothing more.***")

"How intimate can I get with a sister?" As intimate as you'd get with your own human sister—and nothing more!

> Flee also youthful lusts. (2 Tim 2:22 KJV)
>
> Give no opportunity to the devil. (Eph 4:27 RSV)

Can you see the wisdom of our loving heavenly Father in these directives? He created woman to be more affected by touch—"It is good for a man not to *touch* a woman" (1 Cor 7:1 KJV). He created man to be more affected by sight—"Every one who looks at a woman lustfully has already committed adultery with her in his heart" (Matt 5:28 RSV).

Therefore, in order to protect us, his children, from starting on a path that leads to inevitable disaster (either immediately or eventually), he gives us a spiritual traffic signal and says: "I don't want you getting frustrated and I don't want you exploiting one another. I also don't want you getting in a position where you always have to go a little farther for the same kicks you got the night before. So, to say it simply—cool it."

Remember:

> The eyes of the Lord are in every place, keeping watch on the evil and the good. (Prov 15:3 RSV)

And if some young fellow hands you the old line, "If you love me, you will; if you don't, you'll lose me," ask yourself, "If I do lose him, have I lost much?" "Love is... never selfish or rude. Love does not demand its own way" (1 Cor 13:5 TLB).

Or how about, "C'mon, everybody is doing it"? To this you can easily respond, "Everybody may be doing it, though that I sort of doubt, but here is one girl who is not going along with the crowd in this particular thing." Keep in mind that though it may seem so at times, the majority is not always right. When Joseph's brothers wanted to get rid of him, one brother said, "Let's not kill him." If the majority had ruled, Joseph would have been killed. But one brother dared stand up for what he believed to be right.

If you ever find yourself in a situation where some

fellow just simply isn't getting the message about "hands off," pray quickly and then slap him firmly. Your biblical basis is "Whatever your hand finds to do, do it with all your might" (Eccles 9:10 RSV).

> For God has not called us for uncleanness, but in holiness. (1 Thess 4:7 RSV)

I can almost hear you right about now—

"Okay, I see it! I know it! I want to do it—but how? Petting. Viewing pornography. Masturbation. Lustful fantasizing. Homosexuality. I don't want to walk in uncleanness, disobey my Lord, lose out on abundant living, experience guilt, defeat and frustration, risk blowing my future—yet how do I break free?!"

Listen closely. *Satan's cover is about to be blown!*

There is only one way to walk in purity and victory as a believer: *we must win the battle for our minds.*

"Huh?"

That's right—win the battle for our minds.

Satan's chief objective is to control our minds. He knows that we are the product of our thinking and if he can manipulate our thought life, he can control our actions.

"But I fear, lest by any means, as the serpent beguiled Eve through his subtlety, *so your minds* should be corrupted from the simplicity that is in Christ" (2 Cor 11:3 KJV).

The secret to dealing with our actions is to deal with our thoughts. That is where sin begins—in the thought life. If you deal with sin in the realm of the thoughts, the actions will take care of themselves. (Please read that again.)

Sow a thought—reap an act. Sow an act—reap a habit. Sow a habit—reap a lifestyle. Sow a lifestyle—reap a destiny.

The thought itself is not sin. It is simply temptation to sin. *We can't help who knocks on the door of our mind, but we can decide whom we want to let in and whom we want to entertain.*

To deal with sin we've got to take the Western approach: "Head it off at the pass!" At all costs, get rid of the thought!

Therefore, if we are going to walk in purity as Christians, we have to win the battle for our minds. If you do not consciously control every thought going through your head, the resulting slackness makes it "cake" for Satan to introduce his own ideas. (You may not be aware that he does this, for the thoughts appear as your own.) An undisciplined thought-life makes you a "sitting duck" for the devil.

> For the weapons of our warfare are not carnal, but mighty through God to the *pulling down of strongholds; Casting down imaginations,* and every high thing that exalteth itself against the knowledge of God, and *bringing into captivity every thought* to the obedience of Christ. (2 Cor 10:4-5 KJV)

Notice it says, "*every thought.*"

A raunchy thought comes crawling across your mind. If you don't "bring it into the captivity of Christ" (rejecting it according to Christ and His Word), that thought can become a "stronghold" (hold onto you with a strong hold), produce "imaginations," and then lead you to the sinful action.

It also says "warfare."

Many Christians are not aware of our spiritual warfare—warfare with the one whom Jesus said wants to "steal, and to kill and to destroy" us (John 10:10 KJV). We can't sit back and be passive hoping, "If I don't bother him maybe he won't bother me." "Sin lieth (Hebrew, lurks, like an animal) at the door (Gen 4:7a KJV) its desire is for you, but you must master it" (Gen 4:7b RSV).

"*Be strong in the Lord* and in the strength of his might. *Put on the whole armor of God,* that you may be able to *stand against* the wiles (Satan's favorite wile is "wait awhile!") of the devil. For we are not *contending against* flesh and blood, but *against* the principalities, *against* the powers, *against* the world rulers of this present darkness, *against* the spiritual hosts of wickedness in the heavenly places. Therefore, *take the whole armor of God,* that you may be able to *withstand* in the evil day, and having done all, to stand (Eph 6:10-13 RSV).

Are you standing strong as a soldier in the army of our Lord waging war against the enemy and daily emerging as an overcomer?

Or are you wallowing in defeat whimpering because you've latched on to lies Satan has stuffed into your head like—"I can't overcome this habit" or "Satan's got me. I'll never get the victory"?

I charge you right now in the name of Jesus Christ our Lord to put your foot down and stop genuflecting to the devil. Jesus defeated him 2,000 years ago!

> For this purpose the Son of God was manifested, that he might destroy the works of the devil. (1 John 3:8 KJV)

Already Satan has been crushed under the Lord's feet. Now Jesus wants us to consummate the victory by putting him under *our* feet.

> . . . then the God of peace will soon crush Satan under your feet. (Rom 16:20 RSV)

If you're tired of being Satan's Pinocchio, with him pulling the strings and manipulating you to walk in uncleanness, then repent of your passive attitude and look him right in the eye saying, "From this day forward I make a decision to walk in purity by believing and obeying the Word of God."

Here are the specifics:

1. *Make a covenant with your eyes.* Job said, "I have made a covenant with my eyes; how then could I look upon a virgin?" (Job 31:1 RSV). ("Look" or "*gaze*" in Hebrew means "to separate mentally.") In other words, no more undressing with your eyes or "separating mentally" the clothes from another's body. Jesus said, "The *eye* is the lamp of the body" (gateway to your mind) (Matt 6:22 TAB). Stay away from all phony stimulants (i.e., any skin magazines, pictures, books, TV programs, movies, videos, newspaper movie ads, etc.) that can engrave impure impressions upon your mind. "I will not set before my eyes *anything* that is base" (Ps 101:3 RSV). "Whatsoever things are *pure* . . . think on these things" (Phil 4:8 KJV). "Touch not the unclean thing" (2 Cor 6:17 KJV). "Make no provision for [indulging] the flesh—put a stop to thinking about the evil cravings of your physical nature—to [gratify its] desires (lusts)" (Rom 13:14 TAB). "Brace up your minds" (1 Pet 1:13 TAB).

Remember "garbage in—garbage out." Don't you dare cry out to God that you're "trapped" in masturbation, lustful fantasizing, etc.—if you're continuing to pollute your mind with visual poison. ("But I view it as beautiful art")—baloney! God discerns "the thoughts and intentions of the heart" (Heb 4:12 RSV) and knows your true motivation. (Someone has said "porno" is material "to be read or seen with one hand," that is, as an accompaniment to masturbation.) If you doubt—do without. "Whatever is not of faith is sin" (Rom 14:23 KJV).

2. *Appropriate by faith your liberation from the power of sin.* Jesus came to provide us not only forgiveness of sin but liberation from its power. Although it may seem incomprehensible to your natural mind, the Word of God teaches that we have been totally "freed from sin" (Rom 6:7 KJV). *We have the ability to sin but no longer the obligation.* This is a fact in the mind of God and it is not changed by whether we believe it or not. (A long time ago I stopped saying "God said it. I believe it. That settles it." Now I say, "God said it. That settles it!")

Read Romans 6:1-22: "That we might no longer be enslaved to sin." . . . "Freed from sin." . . . "Sin will have no dominion over you." . . . "Set free from sin." . . . "You have been set free from sin." Our trouble is that we've been a slave to sin for so long that when the "good news" now comes to us, deep down inside we really don't believe it. This is like the slave who had served for forty years who was told that Lincoln had issued the "Emancipation Proclamation" and he would soon be free. He couldn't believe it initially but as he walked around repeating in disbelief, "I've been set free? I've been set free?"—it finally hit him. "Whoopee, I really have been set free!"

The same thing will happen to us. It just takes awhile for the truth to sink from our minds into our spirits and explode in all its glory.

> I don't have to serve sin today . . . for I have been *set free!*

For two years I had this scriptural statement on my hallway mirror. I'd confess it daily. It's Romans 6:6-7 personalized for my edification. Little by little my mind was renewed to believe this fact. Finally, after about three months, the reality of this verse hit me like an atomic explosion. I've never been the same. I'd encourage you to read Romans 6 in your Bible (the Christian's Magna Carta) and do as I did with this verse. It's really true—We Don't Have to Be Sin's Slave! We are to walk in the "glorious liberty of the children of God" (Rom 8:21 KJV).

3. *Follow the instructions in the Manufacturer's Handbook.*

> Submit yourselves therefore to God. Resist the devil and he will flee. (James 4:7 RSV)

"Submit to God"—when you recognize that the tempter is tempting you (Tip-off: Our thoughts are in direct contradiction to what we know is God's will), humble yourself immediately. Make a quick, silent phone call to Glory: "Lord, I'm helpless in my own strength. I need you." Always remember:

> Not by might, nor by power, but by my Spirit, says the Lord of hosts. (Zech 4:6 RSV)

Don't hesitate for a second. If you allow Satan to get his foot in the door, he'll come in and destroy the whole house.

Don't feel embarrassed due to the nature of the thought. Jesus knows what it's like:

> Therefore, He had to be made like his brethren in all things, that He might become a merciful and faithful high priest in things pertaining to God, to make propitiation for the sins of the people. For since He Himself was tempted in that which He has suffered, He is able to come to the aid of those who are tempted. (Heb 2:17-18 NAS)

"You mean Jesus was tempted sexually? Do you think he struggled with sexual sins?"

Without a doubt. That's why he, as our older brother, can so identify with what we're going through.

> For we do not have a high priest who cannot sympathize with our weaknesses, but one who has been tempted in all things as we are, yet without sin. (Heb 4:15-16 NAS)

"Resist the devil and he will flee." We're not told to resist temptation, but the tempter. How? Using the mighty name of Jesus (Mark 16:17) and taking up the one offensive weapon listed in Ephesians 6.

> Take . . . the sword of the Spirit, which is the word of God. (Eph 6:17 RSV)
>
> For the weapons of our warfare are not carnal but

> mighty through God to the pulling down of strongholds. (2 Cor 10:4 KJV)

Fighting off Satan's attacks with carnal weapons is like a soldier trying to deflect bullets with his fists. The Word is our mighty weapon. The Word spoken in faith by a believer is dynamite!

When Jesus resisted Satan in the wilderness he used the same weapon that we are called to use—the Word of God. Three times he said, "It is written" (Matt 4:1-10). The result was the same as it will be for us (when we operate in faith): "Then the devil left him" (Matt 4:11 RSV).

Say, "Satan, I rebuke you in the name of the Lord Jesus Christ, for it is written—"

> Whosoever shall call on the name of the Lord shall be delivered. (Joel 2:32 KJV)
>
> Ye are of God, little children, and have overcome them: because greater is he that is in you, than he that is in the world. (1 John 4:4 KJV)
>
> No temptation has overtaken you that is not common to man. God is faithful, and he will not let you be tempted beyond your strength, but with the temptation will also provide the way of escape, that you may be able to endure it. (1 Cor 10:13 RSV).
>
> . . . Young men, because you are strong, and the word of God abides in you, and you have overcome the evil one. (1 John 2:14 RSV)

These are just a few examples of verses I have used almost daily over the years. Dig out some others and have an entire arsenal ready! (1 Corinthians 10:13 is definitely one to commit to memory.)

"Draw near to God and he will draw near to you" (James 4:8).

Praise God for the victory *even though you may still feel the "heat" of Satan's attack.* Remember "a double-minded man" will receive nothing from the Lord" (James 1:8). *You must act in faith.* "Without faith it is impossible to please him. For whoever would draw near to God must believe that *he exists* and that *he rewards* those who seek him" (Heb 11:6 RSV).

> What things soever ye desire, *when ye pray,* believe that ye receive them, and ye shall have them. (Mark 11:24 KJV)

In other words, you have to believe you've got it before you get it! Here's how you receive from the Lord:

1. *Desire*—"What things soever you desire . . ."
2. *Decision*—". . . when you pray, *believe* that you have received them. . . ."
3. *Determination*—". . . and you shall have them." (Patience)

Notice the last word—"patience." Many underestimate its importance, but patience is what undergirds your faith. Like "salt and pepper," faith and patience work as a dynamic duo to see you through the temptation or test to ultimate victory.

. . . through *faith* and *patience* inherit the promises (Heb 6:12 RSV).

"Patience" means to:

1. persevere
2. remain steadfast and never give in
3. endure
4. stay behind or under

Patience is not:

1. knuckling under
2. hanging on
3. resignation

"What if I slip?"

The most important move you will ever make as a Christian is the move you make right after you fail. Remember when sin is not confessed but excused, we open up a door for bondage (John 8:34). So move quickly and be honest. God's Word doesn't change. Neither does his love for you. Pick yourself up, confess and forsake your sin, then move on. For years I've had a motto, "Confess and move on!" Here's a good Scripture to use as well:

> Forgetting what lies behind . . .
> Reaching for what lies ahead . . .
> Pressing on toward the goal. (Phil 3:13-14)

It's glorious that the same loving Lord who gives us clear directives on love, sex and marriage, also gives us the necessary grace to emerge successfully—"as kings in life."

> Those who receive God's overflowing grace and the free gift of righteousness reign as kings in life through the One, Jesus Christ. (Rom 5:17 TAB)

"Why wait til marriage?" First of all, then, because God commands it. The remaining two reasons simply flow from this more important one.

You Reap What You Sow in the Present.

"AAAWWWwwwhhh—splat!"

"Why did that guy jump out of that towering building? What was he—crazy?"

"I don't know. All I heard him yell was that he didn't believe in the law of gravity, then he jumped."

"Didn't he know that whether a person believes in the law or not—it still holds?"

"I dunno—guess he really must've been *deceived.*"

Our Lord created the world to be subject to certain physical laws. Likewise, he has established specific spiritual laws which are equally essential to the well-being of his creation. We are deceived when we believe we can ignore these laws without serious consequences.

One spiritual law which is probably the most important one for us is called the "law of sowing and reaping."

> Do not be deceived; God is not mocked, for whatever a man sows, that he will also reap. (Gal 6:7 RSV)
>
> Don't be misled; remember that you can't ignore God and get away with it: a man will always reap just the kind of crop he sows. (Gal 6:7 TLB)

In the physical realm it works like this: Sow corn and you'll reap corn (not onions). Sow carrots and you'll reap carrots (not bananas). Simple enough, isn't it? First the physical, and then the spiritual (1 Cor 15:46).

In the spiritual realm it works like this: *sow obedience* to the laws of God and you'll *reap the benefits. Sow disobedience* to the laws of God and you'll *reap the consequences.* Obedience equals benefits; disobedience equals consequences. Really profound, huh?

In discussing our subject, we've cited that so-called "free-love" is really a misnomer. It's like "Grape-nuts"—neither "grapes" nor "nuts." In "free love" a person is free to defy God but not free to escape the consequences. With the "kick" comes the inevitable "kickback."

"Be sure your sin will find you out" (Num 32:23 RSV).

"He who despises the word brings destruction on himself, but he who respects the commandment will be rewarded" (Prov 13:13 RSV).

"Blessed is the man who fears the Lord always; but he who hardens his heart will fall into calamity" (Prov 28:14 RSV).

"He who digs a pit will fall into it, and a stone will come back upon him who starts it rolling" (Prov 26:27 RSV).

While sowing obedience to the Word of God in the realm of sexuality brings untold blessings both now and for the rest of one's life, sowing disobedience brings consequences from which one *cannot* escape. They may not all occur, but some will occur. They may not happen immediately, but they will happen eventually.

"Do not be deceived; God is not mocked, for whatever a man sows that he will also reap" (Gal 6:7 RSV).

Evidence of the "blindness" Scripture speaks of for those not under the Lordship of Jesus is clearly seen in our present paganistic society which has "chucked" the laws of God almost wholesale, is reaping the crop it has sown, yet seems unable or unwilling to make the connection. Twenty years of so-called "liberation" and the "new morality" has brought astronomical increases in divorce, abortion, illegitimate childbirth, teen-age pregnancy, homosexuality, AIDS, herpes, pornography and suicide, not to mention the shattered families left in the dust. One hundred years ago only one in thirty-two families experienced divorce. Today it is rapidly approaching one in two. And if the family goes, so goes the society. Nineteen of twenty-one civilizations have fallen apart, not from external attack but from within (moral collapse). Is this the direction we're headed?

Decades ago during the communist revolution in Russia, an attempt was made to eliminate the biblical concept of sexuality and marriage. Legal restraints against "free-love" were removed. Premarital sex, rather than being condemned, was accepted and even encouraged by the state.

The results of this new morality? Instead of strengthening the state, it seemed to be destroying its very fiber. Shortly thereafter, the Russians reverted back to their former standards. Atheistic Russia confronted a spiritual law: whatever a man sows, that will he also reap.

How about *you*? Have you let Satan deceive you into thinking that your way is right even though it directly contradicts the Word of God?

"The way of a fool is right in his own eyes, but he that hearkeneth unto counsel is wise" (Prov 12:15 KJV).

Consider these words from David Wilkerson in his message, "Parked at the Gates of Hell":

"Who but God could know what goes on in parked cars and secluded woods across this nation? Who but

God could see what happens on nights like this when students test their moral courage and their codes; who but God could really know what sweethearts are allowing in their lives; what privileges are being demanded; what risks are being taken; who but God could see the whole picture? The Bible warns, 'Can a man take fire in his bosom and not be burned?'

"Young people break the laws of God and then excuse it by saying, 'God made me this way; we're only doing what comes naturally; we're in love; God will forgive us anyhow; God knows our human weaknesses; he knows our hearts.' It can happen so quickly; it can even happen on the way home from a religious service such as this. Too suddenly, in a frenzy of hugging and kissing and petting, the natural flame that God has put in the heart of every young man and woman begins to burn out of control before God's appointed time and without God's approval; and the devil keeps urging you on and whispering, 'It's all right—you're in love, you belong to each other, you have a right—and even if you get into trouble he will carry you through, he'll stick with you, she'll stick with you—everything's all right!'

"These stolen pleasures last only for a very short time, and then the roof caves in. One minute it can seem so right and pretty and so good because the devil can bring two young people together and make everything seem so pure and sweet and clean, when in actuality their lives are going through the filth and dirt and exceeding sinfulness of sin. Then as the pleasure ebbs away and the emotions are brought under control, it becomes dirty, wrong and sordid. One moment you thought it was real love, and the next you saw it for what it really was. It is then that these two realize they have parked right at the gates of hell and allowed Satan to deceive them."

What are some consequences one can reap in the *present* if he or she sows disobedience to God in the areas covered by this book?

Loss of virginity.

Teen pregnancy.

Forced marriage (one out of two "teen marriages" fail within a few years).

Abortion.

Physical damage from an abortion.

Sexually transmitted diseases.

Divorce.

Suicide. (The majority of suicide cases are reported to be girls under thirty.)

These are some of the more obvious consequences of disobeying the laws of God and becoming physically involved before marriage. Yet some "clever" people still think they can "mock God" by using premarital birth control, twisting the Scriptures, listening to liberal "authorities," "doing everything but," etc. They too will reap what they sow as there are other "less obvious," yet equally destructive, consequences that no one can escape.

Guilt—Millions of people today feel depressed ("pressed down") but don't know why. Depression is not really the problem: *guilt* is and this comes from breaking God's laws. *Guilt results in depression.* Satan uses guilt to condemn and accuse us and lure us to unbiblical forms of relief—booze, dope, Valium, constant partying, the occult, illicit sex, etc. But none work except for a short while.

"He that keepeth the law, happy is he" (Prov 29:18 KJV). "But the wicked are like the troubled sea, when it cannot rest, whose waters cast up mire and dirt. There is no peace, saith my God, to the wicked" (Isa 57:20-21 KJV). God uses guilt to firmly "press down" upon us that we might employ the privilege of confession and cleansing of the conscience. This is an important spiritual law—"He who *conceals* his transgressions will not prosper (Hebrew, go ahead), but he who *confesses and forsakes* them will obtain mercy" (Prov 28:13 RSV).

> Blessed is he whose transgression is forgiven, whose sin is covered. Blessed is the man to whom the Lord imputes no iniquity, and in whose spirit there is no deceit. When I declared not my sin, my body wasted away through my groaning all day long. For day and night thy hand was heavy upon me; my strength was dried up as by the heat of summer. I acknowledged my sin to thee, and I did not hide my iniquity; I said, "I will confess my transgressions to the Lord"; then thou didst forgive the guilt of my sin. (Ps 32:1-5 RSV)

Our conscience serves as the red light on the dashboard to alert us of our need for correcting wrong behavior. What must one do to set his conscience at rest? Not take a hammer and smash the red light! The problem is not with the dashboard light; it merely warns that something needs to be checked under the hood.

So too, if our conscience "lights up" and feelings of depression follow, it's time to "check under the hood" to correct, not cover the problem.

Remember: "Do right and you'll feel right."

Flashbacks—"Instant replays" in the mind of sexual

experiences is a favorite trick of the enemy to draw us into lustful thoughts, masturbation, loss of sleep, etc. (If this is presently happening to you even though you've repented, pray for the person pictured when Satan "rolls the film." Then begin to meditate on the Word or sing praise to his name.)

Dear Larry,

I was really blessed with a teaching you gave in November and I wanted to share with you a little of what happened and to thank you for what that teaching has done in helping my Christian walk. Your talk was on "Why wait til marriage?" and, at the end, you asked us to make a commitment in purity by God's grace and even to write down this commitment in our Bibles. I remember that you said something like in three years we would rejoice at making this commitment now. Well, it has only been a month and a half and I already see God blessing me through that commitment.

The talk was excellently timed for me because I was struggling with a similar question that night. A guy I had dated two years ago had come to see me just the week before and we started talking about the fact that we still felt a physical attraction to each other and, unfortunately, talking about it led to some light petting which I was very upset about later. I *knew* in my mind that it was wrong but did not do a very good job of resisting Satan that day. This had happened a couple of times before with this guy and each time I said it would not happen again—but it did.

I know God wanted me to hear your message that

Tuesday because it was the first time I'd been there in about three months; I go to school too far to make it every week.

You seemed to describe me perfectly when you said that there would be "reruns" because *I couldn't get it out of my mind.* I hurt so much inside because of my disobedience to God. When you asked us to make a commitment to walk in purity I didn't feel like I could but I knew that I should, so I did.

Since then I have been shown some real things about God and His love for me and also my future to realize that I want to keep this commitment because I know it's what God wants. I did some realistic thinking on my friendship with this guy and saw that our friendship was not glorifying to God and I have felt that the best way to be a real friend is to pull back from seeing him and pray for him. Thank you for your teaching, Larry. I feel released from a bondage.

A sister in Christ,
Sue

Some other consequences one can reap in the present are:

Bondage—Petting outside of the marriage relationship, like all immediate satisfactions of the flesh, is subject to a moral law of diminishing returns. The more one gets, the more one wants. In time, the more one gets, the less one enjoys what is gotten. Yet those who pet are faced with a habitual necessity for releasing sexual tension. Once a relationship degenerates to the point at which petting becomes "a way to express our 'love' for each other," the two find engaging in this immediate pleasure becomes all-absorbing and, pretty soon, a routine. The relationship seems to depend for its success on the petting that has now become a demand. The tone of the relationship deteriorates. Selfish exploitation rules. The spirit is sadly conscious of the fact that what seemed so "wonderful" at first has now become a bondage to the flesh. The words of Jesus bring teardrops in the night, "Truly, truly, I say to you, every one who commits sin is the slave of sin" (John 8:34 NAS).

Loss of reputation and self-respect—Fear of being discovered in sin is bad enough, but the problem goes even deeper. You begin to entertain gnawing thoughts, "What would others think of me if they knew? Will I get the reputation of being an easy make? Why do I feel so cheap? I wish I never had . . ."

"A good name is rather to be chosen than great riches" (Prov 22:1 KJV).

Separation from God—Paul in Romans 8 asks, "What can separate me from the love of God?" Pressure? Persecution? Circumstances? There is *only one thing* and this is only temporary because of Calvary—

> Behold the Lord's hand is not shortened, that it cannot save, or his ear dull, that it cannot hear; but your iniquities have made a separation between you and your God, and your sins have hid his face from you so that he does not hear. (Isa 59:1-2 RSV)

It is futile to pray to the Lord for anything, and I do mean anything, if one is walking in sin. It is a clear *fact* of Scripture—not only will he not answer, but he doesn't even hear your prayer! "If I had cherished iniquity in my heart, *the Lord would not have listened*" (Ps 66:18 RSV).

This, more than any other reason, should propel us back into the mainstream of his will. Heaven forbid that there ever be a blockage in our lines of communication with our heavenly Father.

You Reap What You Sow in the Future

The third reason why we should wait til marriage is the fact that we will reap in the future what we sow today—either benefits or consequences.

"Cast your bread upon the waters, for you will find it after many days" (Eccles 11:1 RSV).

At present, my wife, Doris, and I are reaping the *benefits* of what we sowed prior to our marriage. That doesn't mean we didn't struggle with keeping pure (remember what I said about a "400 horsepower engine in a VW body"?). But we were able to walk up that aisle, look in one another's eyes, and know that by the grace of God we had remained pure. Since that day I can honestly say we are experiencing God's intention in marriage: "days of heaven upon the earth" (Deut 11:21 KJV). Praise be to his name!

But what are some of the consequences reaped *in the future* for sowing disobedience today?

Marry the wrong person—That's right. There is no other area in life where one had better be sure he has "the mind of the Lord" than in the selection of a life partner. Yet if one chooses to walk in disobedience to God, thereby cutting himself or herself off from answered prayer (Isa 59:1-2), there is absolutely no assurance of selecting the one God intended. It's as simple as this: *If you want to know God's choice, you must be able to hear God's voice.*

Sexual dysfunction in marriage—Why are millions

today frustrated in their marital sex life? Women find it difficult or seem unable to respond. Likewise with men. Sex therapists and psychiatrists offer their "sophisticated" solutions: Sex manuals, pornography, wife-swapping, having an affair, etc.—yet none of these seem to work. What's up?

Here's the deception: "Good sexual adjustment makes for a good marriage." This is also used to promote living together before marriage because supposedly, "practice of a couple's sex life produces a good marriage."

Brothers and sisters, this is a bold-faced lie straight from the pit of hell! It is *not* "good sexual adjustment makes for a good marriage" but ***"a good marriage makes for good sexual adjustment."*** And a good marriage has at least three distinct elements: the physical, the "soulish" (or psychological), and the spiritual, with your mind being your most important sex organ. A truly good sexual relationship demands and involves all you are as a person.

Suppose that prior to marriage you flagrantly defy God's laws. You learn about sex in an atmosphere that is shy and secret, watchful, hurried, scared of interruption. This is sex *learned with guilt.* (Even if you're not in this type of atmosphere, guilt is still inevitable because God designed it as an automatic accompaniment to sin.) Initially you get used to holding yourself back, then you try to convince yourself it's okay. ("I gotta get rid of these dumb feelings. *Cosmo* and *Playboy* say they're just 'sexual hang-ups from my religious upbringing.'") What happens? Programmed into your subconscious are the "guilt experiences." Later in marriage they surface, "Why can't I let go? . . . respond? . . . what's blocking?"

Recently I spoke with a man of God who has taught

and counseled in the area of love, sex and marriage for over twenty years. He said that he repeatedly confronts the problem of, "We engaged in premarital sex and derived much pleasure, yet now something is wrong." He said the same reason surfaces in almost every case: before marriage the couple constantly hesitated yet succumbed. Now the girl subconsciously feels she was robbed of her virginity. The guy subconsciously feels that he was somehow "caught" or "trapped" into the marriage. A subconscious resistance interferes with their normal sexual enjoyment and they are in need of the supernatural healing power of Jesus.

Remember: You can't always determine the rightness or wrongness of an action by what happens *immediately* but by what happens *eventually*.

Other consequences reaped in the future are:

Elimination of perfect trust in marriage—If you engage in sexual experimentation before you commit yourselves publicly to each other in marriage, how can you be sure you'll stay trusting each other later? If you jump the fence prior to marriage and disregard God's moral laws, who's to say you or your partner won't do the same thing after you're married? What you do lays a foundation for distrust after the wedding.

A friend of mine who is a stewardess mentioned how she notices so many businessmen who have faint marks on their fingers where their wedding rings belong. They conveniently remove them when they are away from their wives.

Do you want to spend your married life in fear forever wondering if. . . . ?

Perfect love casts out fear. (1 John 4:18 RSV)

Problems related to self-control—Do you know the number one reason why marriages break up? "Sexual problems?" "Financial problems?" No. The chief reason is simply: Lack of self-control. If a person can't control himself—sexual problems arise. If a person can't control himself—financial problems arise. Temper problems. On and on it goes.

Often in marriage one must forego the sex act because of "battling sickness," pregnancy, travel, or some other situation. Only the self-controlled individual can cope.

The time period before marriage is our loving Lord's "developing ground" for cultivating this fruit of the Spirit in our lives. Disregard it and repercussions can be felt for the rest of one's life.

> A man without self-control is like a city broken into and left without walls. (Prov 25:28 RSV)

Severely damaging the personality of another—God puts limits on the display of affection before marriage because he knows the delicate emotional make-up of a woman as the "weaker vessel" (1 Pet 3:7). If a couple is physically intimate with one another and then the fellow decides he wants to break it off, severe mental and emotional trauma can be experienced by the woman. She feels she has "given herself" to her man and now feels rejected and betrayed. America is full of women who feel they've been betrayed somewhere by a man and as a result distrust men. (This is the basis for much of the "Women's Liberation" movement.)

My sister who went with a fellow for over four years flew into a tailspin when he "broke off their relationship." She became hate-filled, started drinking over fourteen drinks a night and gained sixty-five pounds in one year (til she met the Lord Jesus). I watched my sister almost totally devastated by this severed relationship. Breaking off is hard enough in this type of normal situation, let alone between a couple who has been intimately involved.

Need any more be said?

The Bible speaks of those who are "ever learning and never coming into knowledge." In other words, people who are ever evaluating, considering but never reaching any decision and acting upon it.

As your brother in Jesus, I want to ask you to now act upon what you've just heard. I'd like to ask you to do something that I did years ago and have been thankful for ever since. (I still have the paper on which it appears.)

Will you join with me and millions of other disciples of Jesus Christ in committing yourself to walk in purity "in the midst of a wicked and perverse generation"?

Will you commit yourself to settle for nothing but the best in terms of what God has intended in your life?

Jesus desires to smash the meaningless and worldly counterfeits by raising up a kingdom counterculture to be a model of "his better way."

Will you accept the challenge?

My Decision

"Lord Jesus, by your grace and the power of your Holy Spirit, I commit myself today to walk in purity for the glory of your Name."

Signed ______________________________

Date ______________________________

FIVE

The Christian Alternative: Friendship

WHAT WOULD YOU THINK if I told you that the term "dating" doesn't even appear in the Bible?

"Huh?"

That's right—not even once!

"Well—ah—ah—"

What would you think if I told you that the three reasons usually stated for dating—companionship, learning to relate with members of the opposite sex, and mate selection—have already been provided for in our kingdom counterculture? The body of Christ offers these benefits (and in such a way as to eliminate many of the pitfalls!).

"Huh! Are you saying that dating is . . . is . . . sin?"

Hold your socks on. That's not what I'm saying. Nowhere does the Bible say, "Thou shalt not date" but neither does it say "Thou shalt." The intention of this last chapter is to present a Christian alternative to those who are looking for a healthy, satisfying way of developing relationships—first with members of their own sex, then with members of the opposite sex.

"What's it called?"

Friendship. And it's patterned after the One who said:

> I have called you friends. (John 15:15 RSV)

Before we dig in, let's touch base on a few very important introductory points.

1. *Our Lord does not want us getting all bent out of shape trying to discover our life partners. He wants us to first find rest and security in our relationship with him.* Walking around nervously like a turkey while going through the mental gymnastics of looking for our "phantom hero" with our sixteen point check-list (check, check, check, check, oh—doesn't measure up—start again—check, check, check) is not only frustrating but a clever tool of the enemy to get our eyes off Jesus. May I remind you that "God brought the woman to the man." Adam didn't have to go beat down the bushes! Jesus doesn't want us goin' bananas inside about our life partners. Remember his Words:

> Come to me, all who labor and are heavy laden, and I will give you *rest.* (Matt 11:28 RSV)

For you right now, the important question is not: "Will I ever be married?" It's a two part query: "What is God's will for my life now?" and then "Do I want God's will?"

"But I have to hurry. I might become an old prune!" or "Me a bachelor til the rapture!"

"He who makes haste with his feet misses his way" (Prov 19:2 RSV).

Rest easy. He knows the right time. *It would be far better* to be single, in the will of God, and experience some loneliness than to be married, out of the will of God, and experience chaos. Besides, no person has the right to ask another person to enter into their confusion!

When we got married, I was 26; Doris, 25. I can honestly say that if we had gotten married just one year earlier, our life would have been a mess. That's right. Our loving Lord knew *exactly* when we were ready and brought just the right people, circumstances, and teaching our way to prepare us in the year before the big day. The verse God gave Doris and me was, "Prepare your work outside, get everything ready for you in the field; and after that build your house" (Prov 24:27 RSV).

Why don't you do as I did years ago? Lay it on the altar by praying "Father, when you think I can serve you better and be happier married, you bring the right person my way. Til then I'll serve you with all my heart, obeying your will for my life."

"And what is his will for my life?"

It's revealed in 1 Thessalonians 5:16-18. (Maybe now you'll see why he feels you're just not quite ready yet!) "For this is the will of God in Christ Jesus for you":

1. Rejoice always.
2. Pray constantly.
3. Give thanks in all circumstances.

Now's your chance to be a "doer of the Word"!

2. *"Do not be unequally yoked up with unbelievers—do not make mismated alliances with them, or come under a different yoke with them [inconsistent with your faith].* For what partnership have right living and right standing

with God with iniquity and lawlessness? Or how can light fellowship with darkness? . . . So, come out from among (unbelievers), and separate (sever) yourselves from them, says the Lord, and touch not [any] unclean thing; then I will receive you kindly and treat you with favor, and I will be a Father to you, and you shall be My sons and daughters, says the Lord Almighty" (2 Cor 6:14, 17, 18, TAB).

God states very clearly here that a Christian is not to be yoked with a nonbeliever. Though most people try to apply this to marriage, a close examination of this passage reveals that marriage is not even remotely in the context of the passage. Being "yoked" is more likely to mean any relationship in which the nonbeliever can become a mixing or diluting influence upon our lives.

"So shun youthful passions and aim at righteousness, faith, love, and peace, *along with those who call upon the Lord from a pure heart*" (2 Tim 2:22 RSV).

> Run from anything that gives you the evil thoughts that young men often have, but stay close to anything that makes you want to do right. Have faith and love, and *enjoy the companionship of those who love the Lord and have pure hearts.* (2 Tim 2:22 TLB)
>
> "Bad company ruins good morals" (1 Cor 15:33 RSV).
>
> "Can two walk together, except they be agreed?" (Amos 3:3)
>
> "And if a house is divided against itself, that house will not be able to stand" (Mark 3:25 RSV).
>
> "He who is not with me is against me" (Matt 12:30 RSV).

"He who walks with wise men becomes wise, but the companion of fools will suffer harm" (Prov 13:20 RSV).

"By rejecting conscience, certain persons have made shipwreck of their faith" (1 Tim 1:19 RSV).

God's people under the old covenant were forbidden to take foreign wives (Deut 7:3). Repeatedly they disobeyed this commandment and thereby suffered the judgment of God (see Ezra 10). The New Testament tells us that a Christian is only to marry another Christian. "A wife is bound to her husband as long as he lives. If the husband dies, she is free to be married to whom she wishes, *only in the Lord"* (1 Cor 7:39 RSV). "Only in the Lord" means only to a Christian and in accordance with God's specific will.

Genesis 24:1-4 told the people of God not to take Canaanites for spouses. Someone has said a Canaanite is someone who is selfish and lives to please himself. The word looks like "canine." In other words, a relationship with a Canaanite is puppy love and can be a prelude to a dog's life!

So as a sister in the Lord you ask, "But how do I turn down 'dates' with unbelievers? Or how do I disengage myself from a relationship with one?"

Don't reject the person. Just get totally involved for Jesus. Encourage him or her to come along. If he does, he'll be drawn closer to the Lord. If he refuses, he'll eliminate himself. As he walks on his own way, the Holy Spirit can convict him as he realizes the caliber of your dedication to Jesus.

So as a brother in the Lord you ask, "But what about all the real good-lookin' girls who are unbelievers?"

> Charm is deceitful, and beauty is vain, but a woman who fears the Lord is to be praised. (Prov 31:30 RSV)

Brothers and sisters, please don't fall flat on this commandment of our Lord. God means it: no missionary dating. I could sit and share with you for hours the names and addresses of disobedient Christians who defiled God in this area, compromised the Word, and since have "gone down the tubes." I mean it. My heart aches even as I write it.

3. *Commitment in a local fellowship of believers is essential, not optional. A necessity, not a luxury.* There is no such thing in the body of Christ as a "Christian grasshopper" or a "spiritual gypsy." God's intention for every one of his children is that we be meaningfully (not mystically) committed to a fellowship of believers where we can practically live out our Christian life.

> And they devoted (Greek, committed) themselves to the apostles' teaching, and to fellowship, to the breaking of bread and the prayers. (Acts 2:42 RSV)

This is our call to fellowship in the body of Christ:

> What we have seen and heard we proclaim to you also, that you also may have fellowship with us; and indeed our fellowship is with the Father, and with His Son, Jesus Christ. (1 John 1:3 NAS)

If you are not presently committed in a Christian fellowship, begin now to pray, then seek your place in the body of Christ. (Note: A cell in the human body that refuses to be committed is called a cancer cell and has to be rooted out!) This is not an elective; it's a command. With pressures surrounding us, we need a supportive environment in order to grow in our Christian lives.

> And let us consider and give attentive, continuous care to watching over one another, studying how we may stir up (stimulate and incite) to love and helpful deeds and noble activities; Not forsaking or neglecting to assemble together [as believers]. (Heb 10:24-25 TAB)

Without being an integral part of a local fellowship of believers, you cannot possibly be saved (in the full sense of the word).

"What?"

That's right! Remember that the word "saved" means more than just "fire insurance" when one dies. It means "to be made whole." That is something intended to be happening right now—in the present.

> You shall call his name Jesus, for he will save his people from their sins. (Matt 1:21 RSV)

> For the word of the cross is folly to those who are perishing, but to us who are *being saved* it is the power of God. (1 Cor 1:18 RSV)

One only becomes "whole" in fellowship—where we learn to live as functioning members of the kingdom counterculture. We learn to stop lying and begin learning how to "speak the truth in love." To stop sinful anger and learn to express it legitimately. To stop stealing and learn to share our time, money and resources with our brothers and sisters. stop worthless talk and learn to encourage. To stop bitterness and learn to forgive. All of these come out of Ephesians 4:17-32 and cannot be learned in one's prayer closet.

Which brings us to God's goal for our lives—

> He predestined [us] to become conformed to the image of His Son. (Rom 8:29 NAS)

With the preceding under our belts, now we're ready to look closely at the Christian alternative to dating: Friendship.

Loneliness is often a theme of contemporary songs.

Remember the classic Beatle song, "Eleanor Rigby"—"all the lonely people, where do they all belong?"

This song depicts people who are lonely. Their condition is usually due to a lack of meaningful sharing with others. No one seems to care. They feel very much alone.

"I look to the right and watch, but there is no one who takes notice of me; no refuge remains to me; no one cares for my soul."

Another hit song?

Not really. Actually it is the cry of a believer from Psalm 142:4.

"No one gives me a passing thought. No one will help me; no one cares a bit what happens to me" (Ps 142:4 TLB).

For decades this verse has been quoted in evangelistic meetings as the plea of one outside of Christ. But upon careful examination one finds that this lament is not coming from an *unbeliever* but actually from a *believer*.

"But I thought believers didn't say things like this! Isn't it all victory and goose bumps once a person comes to the Lord? You know—walkin' down Hallelujah Boulevard?"

Those of us who have been with the Lord for more than twenty-four hours have discovered the opposite: it is "through many tribulations we must enter the kingdom" (Acts 14:22 RSV). Amen? (Or "Oh, me!?")

That is why the Christian life was never intended to be lived alone. Our heavenly Father desires it to be walked out practically with others—with friends.

"Two are better than one, because they have a good reward for their toil. For if they fall, one will lift up his fellow; but woe to him who is alone when he falls and has not another to lift him up" (Eccles 4:9-10 RSV).

The only problem is that while we have many brothers and sisters in the body of Christ, most of us really don't have many genuine friends.

Some of us have been too busy being "spiritual" to cultivate authentic friendships.

"Wanna join us for a little basketball, or go shopping together, or just go for a walk?"

"Sorry—I'm studying the Word."

We forget the fourfold development of Jesus which also applies to our development.

> Jesus increased in wisdom and in stature, and in favor with God and man. (Luke 2:52 RSV)

Others have never truly understood what friendship is from a biblical point of view.

Regardless of where you're at, one of the truths the Holy Spirit is pressing home in this hour is the importance of cultivating *genuine* friendships. As conditions continue to disintegrate in society, increasingly we'll realize how much we need each other. How pregnant with meaning is Romans 12:5: "We are members one of another" (TAB—"mutually dependent on one another").

> Remember that in God's plan men and women need each other. (1 Cor 11:11 TLB)

The following is a list of ten biblical characteristics of friendship. All are modeled by our Lord Jesus in his vertical friendship with us. At the horizontal level, we need to see if we are "following in his steps" in relationships with those around us in the body of Christ. First, with members of our own sex, then with members of the opposite sex.

Group situations, which eliminate the pressures of the solitary "dating game," provide an ideal setting for these characteristics to be cultivated. In the security of the group we are free to "pursue love" (1 Corinthians 13 style) and not feel pressured to "pursue marriage."

> Eagerly pursue and seek to acquire [this] love—make it your aim, your great quest. (1 Cor 14:1 TAB)

In the local church to which I belong, we use this list to develop, examine and strengthen our friendships in the light of the Word. Let it serve as a challenge to you and those with whom you sense a "joining" in the Lord.

Go over it together. See where you stand. Working on friendships is truly a biblical alternative to the dilemma of dating.

One suggestion: Don't try to *force* these. Don't try to *enforce* these. Simply rest in his grace and grow into them under his loving direction.

Ten Biblical Characteristics of Friendship

1. *Friends Are Few.*

"A man of many friends comes to ruin" (Prov 18:24 NAS).

Although we are in covenant with *all* believers in the body of Christ, we need to realize that we can only walk it out *practically* with those to whom we are "knit" by the Holy Spirit. Out of the maturity of these specific friendships will come an integrity and stability that will manifest itself wherever we go in the body of Christ. (Consider Jesus: He had his twelve, his three—Peter, James and John—and even his one—John—whom the Living Bible labels "his best friend.") This is not "exclusivism." This is the only practical way it can ever be done.

Isn't it liberating to know you don't need to have six hundred friends?

Consider this illustration: In a crystal structure—which is the most ordered of all atomic structures—with atoms the same size, the maximum number of atoms that any one can touch is twelve.

2. *A Friend Lays Down His Life.*

"Greater love has no one than this, that one lay down

his life for his friends" (John 15:13 NAS).

Don't just spiritualize this one. ("When the firing squad comes, I will step forward.")

"Laying down one's life" means a willingness to serve another and sacrifice for another instead of serving self. It's the willingness to put another's time and needs ahead of one's own. As usual, it's demonstrated in the "little things"—punctuality, attentive listening, refilling his/her glass at the table, and showing him/her other courtesies.

In a fellowship of believers it also means exercising the spiritual gifts God has given you for the common good.

"You mean 'tongues, prophecy and miracles'?"

Yes, but there are other "less dramatic" gifts of the Spirit that are present in the body of Christ which are often forgotten.

> For as in one body we have many members, and all the members do not have the same function, so we, though many, are one body in Christ, and individually members one of another. Having gifts that differ according to the grace given to us, let us use them. (Rom 12:4-6 RSV)

The Forgotten Gifts of the Spirit

1. *Helps*—supporting, lending a hand.
2. *Acts of Mercy*—offering comfort cheerfully.
3. *Serving*—ministering, running an errand.
4. *Contributing Liberally*—giving.
5. *Administrating*—leading, directing.
6. *Teaching*—instructing.
7. *Exhorting*—encouraging. (1 Cor 12:27)

Serving is the foundation of our Lord's life and the life of his body. God is after a serving spirit. We will never outgrow serving. In fact, it is a gift of the Spirit as seen in the list above. Imagine, the ability to fix cars, help people budget, babysit in a time of need, and simply to do little things for others is a supernatural gift from God! Then one day upon entering marriage we take that servant spirit with us which is the basis for a happy home in Christ.

Remember John the Baptist: "The friend of the bridegroom, who stands and hears him, rejoices greatly at the bridegroom's voice; therefore this joy of mine is now full. *He must increase, but I must decrease*" (John 3:29-30 RSV).

3. *A Friend Really Knows You.*

"I have called you friends, for all that I have heard from my Father I have made known to you" (John 15:15 RSV).

A friend is someone with whom you can be real, transparent, authentic—take off the mask—progressively open up—just be yourself. Someone to whom you can say, "Pray with me; I've got a problem with lust" or "My spouse and I really need help."

This takes time and is "risky living" but nonetheless it is the meaning of James 5:16: "Confess your faults one to another, and pray one for another, that ye may be healed" (KJV).

4. *A Friend Loves Unconditionally.*

"A friend loves at all times, and a brother is born for adversity" (Prov 17:17 RSV).

Recently Billy Graham was asked about Richard Nixon: "I am still his friend. I have not forsaken him. I have met and prayed with him many times." That's *friendship*.

5. *A Friend is Available for Counsel.*

"Oil and perfume make the heart glad, So a man's counsel is sweet to his friend" (Prov 27:9 NAS).

Hearing the voice of the Lord *with* you, not *for* you, is another earmark of a true friend. ("I really don't have any clear guidance for you now, but why don't we fast and pray about it together as a team. What do you say?")

While on the subject of "counsel" let me add a quick word concerning the counsel of our parents. Scripture tells us not to forsake it. "My son, keep your father's commandment, and forsake not your mother's teaching" (Prov 6:20 RSV).

> "Honor your father and mother" (this is the first commandment with a promise), "that it may be well with you and that you may live long on the earth." (Eph 6:2-3 RSV)

6. *A Friend Speaks the Truth in Love.*

"Faithful are the wounds of a friend; profuse are the kisses of an enemy" (Prov 27:6 RSV).

Scripture tells us we are to "walk in the light" with one another in order to enjoy true fellowship (John 1:7). There are a number of friends in my life to whom I've verbalized, "I want to give you permission to walk into my life—adjust me—just please take the cleats off when you do."

We all need someone who loves us enough to tell us the truth about ourselves. Not just what we want to hear, but what we *need* to hear. After all, isn't that why "blind spots" are called what they are?

7. *A Friend Encourages You.*

"For the despairing man there should be kindness from his friend" (Job 6:14 NAS).

Job needed more than what his own wife gave him: "Curse God, and die" (Job 2:9 NAS). Real support, huh?

All of us need encouragement, affirmation, support in our Christian lives. Scripture says it is to come *"daily."*

> But encourage one another day after day, as long as it is still called "Today," lest any one of you be hardened by the deceitfulness of sin. (Heb 3:13 NAS)

D.L. Moody once said, "I've never known God to use a discouraged man."

I believe it. Men and women of God are to be men and women of courage. And from where does it come? It comes from God through his Word and through friends who can encourage ("put courage in") us daily.

Believers are to be a resilient people—"forgetting what lies behind and straining forward to what lies ahead, I press on toward the goal" (Phil 3:13-14 NAS). Yet the truth of the matter is that a cloud of discouragement can "so easily beset us" when we trip up along the way.

We forget it took Edison over ten thousand failures before he invented the electric light bulb. (His response after one of them was the classic: "That's not a mistake, it's an education!")

We forget Lincoln's road to the White House: failed in business in 1831, defeated for legislature in 1832, second failure in business in 1833, suffered nervous breakdown in 1836, defeated for speaker in 1838, defeated for elector in 1840, defeated for Congress in 1843, defeated for Congress in 1848, defeated for Senate in 1855, defeated for Vice President in 1856, defeated for Senate in 1858, elected President in 1860.

We're quick to "throw away our confidence which has a great reward" (Heb 10:35).

Satan, "the accuser of the brethren day and night" (Rev 12:10) knows this and eagerly awaits opportunities to usher us into the darkness of discouragement by his nagging lies and perpetual condemnation. He's like a bothersome mosquito buzzing around our heads: "You blew it! How stupid! Give up! etc."

Probably you heard this story. The devil had an auction sale of all his tools. One by one he let them go—except a last little wedge-shaped tool called discouragement. When asked why he would not part with this one, he replied, "When all the other tools fail, I never fail to wedge my way in with this one."

"Take care, brethren, lest there should be in any one of you an evil, unbelieving heart, in falling away from the living God. But encourage one another day after day, as long as it is still called 'Today,' lest any one of you be hardened by the deceitfulness of sin" (Heb 3:13-14 NAS).

Sin is "deceitful." It can easily cause one to give up, become passive and resign oneself to the situation.

Setbacks can foster an "unbelieving heart." They can cause one to "fall away from the living God" and become ineffective "ambassadors for Christ."

Yet God has a solution! It's sandwiched smack-dab in the middle of this verse! "Encourage one another daily."

Hebrews 10:25 makes it even more relevant—"encouraging one another; and all the more, as you see the day drawing near" (NAS). In other words, the closer it comes to the time of the end, the greater the need for daily encouragement from our friends.

8. *A Friend Will Clash With You.*

"Iron sharpens iron, and one man sharpens another" (Prov 27:17).

Conflict in friendships is not something from which to retreat, it is healthy. It is not a setback but a springboard to greater development of character between two men/women of God.

"Clashing" is inevitable. Friendships will be tested by God to see if they'll hold, if they're truly cemented with the love of Christ.

I view my wife as my number one sheep and as my best friend. Our love over the past years has intensified a hundredfold. I know that one of the prime reasons has been God's allowing us to "rub" against each other every so often. Then we have a choice—withdraw like children, lash out like enemies, or deal with it as loving friends. Opting for the "dealing" has worked in us humility, patience and an understanding of Song of Solomon 8:7: "Many waters cannot quench love, neither can floods drown it."

9. *A Friend is Sensitive to One's Emotional State.*

"Like a madman who throws firebrands, arrows, and death, is the man who deceives his neighbor (same Hebrew word for "neighbor" and "friend") and says, 'I am only joking'" (Prov 26:18-19 RSV).

Simply restated—a friend is sensitive to your sensitive areas. He stays away from put-downs, sarcasm and cruel practical jokes. Scripture gives a good example in Proverbs 27:14 (something for which I was "adjusted"). "He who blesses his neighbor (friend) with a loud voice, rising early in the morning, will be counted as cursing" (RSV).

> Be devoted to one another in brotherly love; give preference to one another in honor. (Rom 12:10 NAS)

10. *A Friend is Loyal.*

"A whisperer separates close friends" (Prov 16:28 RSV).

"He who repeats a matter alienates a friend" (Prov 17:9 RSV).

These verses are self-explanatory in underscoring the dangers of disloyalty. In an hour when "men will betray one another" (Matt 24:10), this characteristic of "loyalty" is crucial.

There we have it—the Christian alternative: friendship. Let's review:

Biblical Characteristics of Friendship

1. Friends are few (Prov 18:24).
2. A friend lays down his life—serves (John 15:13-15, 3:25-30).
3. A friend really knows you (John 15:15).
4. A friend loves unconditionally (Prov 17:17).
5. A friend is available for counsel (Prov 27:9).
6. A friend speaks the truth (Prov 27:6).
7. A friend supports and encourages (Eccles 4:9-10).
8. A friend will clash with you (Prov 27:17).
9. A friend is sensitive to one's emotional state (Prov 26:18-19).
10. A friend is loyal (Prov 16:28; 17:9).

Let me close by asking: "Do you desire friends who demonstrate these kinds of traits?"

Then take these characteristics and ask the Holy Spirit to write them across your heart and the hearts of those around you. Then simply begin to *do* them. As you do, remember the words of the Friend who sticks closer than a brother:

> And as you wish that men would do to you, do so to them. (Luke 6:31 RSV)

Addendum

There are three things
  too wonderful
  for me to understand—
no, four!
How an eagle
  glides through the sky.
How a serpent
  crawls upon a rock.
How a ship
  finds its way across
  the heaving ocean.
The *growth of love*
  between a man
  and a girl.

(Prov 30:18-19 TLB)

For those couples whose love has grown to the point where you mutually sense marriage to be the will of the Lord, please take the following "Scriptural Vows" and begin to meditate on them *daily*. The Bible promises us that we will find "prosperity and success" if we "meditate on the Word" and are "careful to do according to all that is written in it" (Josh 1:8 RSV).

As your wife, by the grace of God,
I vow this day to:

I.

Eph 5:31
1 Cor 7:2
John 17:23
1 Cor 7:10

Go with you, from my father and mother, and become one with you.

A. Have you as my very own husband.

B. Be one with you as the Father is in the Son and the Son in the Father so that our being perfected in unity or oneness in marriage will cause the world to believe that God our Father sent Jesus and loves us as he loves him.

C. Never depart or leave you.

II.

Eph 5:22-25
Titus 2:3-5
Eph 5:33
Gen 3:16
1 Pet 3:6
1 Cor 14:35
1 Cor 7:3

Be subject to you as to the Lord; as the church is to be subject to Christ so I ought to be subject to you in everything.

A. Be sensible, pure, a worker in the home, kind, and subject to you so that the Word of God may not be dishonored.

B. Reverence/respect (defer with courtesy) you, as my head (have a wholesome dread of displeasing you).

C. Have my desire be for you and you shall rule over me.

D. Go to you as my husband for spiritual questions and guidance.

E. Never deprive you of sex except we mutually agree for a time to devote ourselves to prayer.

III.

1 Pet 3:9
1 Pet 3:4
1 Tim 2:10
Prov 31:13
Prov 31:12
1 Tim 3:11
Eph 4:15
Eph 4:26
Heb 13:4

Show you chaste (pure from the heart) and respectful (with awe) behavior.

A. Have a meek and quiet spirit which is precious in the sight of the Lord.
B. With humility of mind regard you as being more important than myself.
C. Look well to the ways of our household and not eat the bread of idleness.
D. Work with my hands for you with delight.
E. Do you good as my husband and not harm all the days of my life.
F. Be dignified—not a gossip—be temperate and faithful in all things.
G. Speak the truth to you in love—never lie—and grow up in Christ.
H. Never let the sun go down on my anger.
I. Hold our marriage bed undefiled.

IV.

Mal 2:14
1 Cor 13:7
Prov 17:17
Rom 12:10
Prov 5:19.

Consider myself your wife by covenant.

A. See you as my friend so I will lay down my life for you.
B. Believe the best about you at all times.
C. Be a friend who will love you at all times.
D. Devote myself to you in love as a friend and give preference to you in honor.
E. Intoxicate you always with my love.

As your husband, by the grace of God,
I vow this day to:

I.

Gen 2:24
Eph 5:31
1 Cor 7:2

Leave my father and mother for you to become one with you.

A. Have you as my very own wife.

B. Be one with you as the Father is in the Son and the Son is in the Father so that our being perfected in unity or oneness in marriage will cause the world to believe that God our Father sent Jesus and loves us as he loves him.

C. Never send or put you away.

II.

Eph 5:23
Eph 5:25
Eph 5:33
Col 3:19
Eph 5:28-29
1 Tim 5:8
1 Cor 7:3-5
1 Tim 3:4
Eph 5:26-27
Eph 5:21
Phil 2:3

Agape-love you just as Christ loves the church and gave himself up for her.

A. Exercise headship and responsibility for you as Christ does for the church.

B. Agape-love you as myself.

C. Agape-love you as my own body and nourish (protect and provide for you) and cherish (cultivate you with care and affection).

D. Never deprive you of sex except we mutually agree for a time to devote ourselves to prayer.

E. Sanctify you to present you without spot or wrinkle that you be holy and blameless.

F. Be subject to you in the fear of Christ.
G. Regard you as more important than myself.

III.

1 Pet 3:7
Eph 4:15
1 Pet 3:9
Eph 4:26
Col 3:19
Heb 13:4

Live considerately with you in an understanding way and grant you honor and value as being precious.

A. Speak the truth to you in agape-love—never lie—and grow up in Christ.
B. Not return evil for evil or insult for insult but give a blessing instead.
C. Never let the sun go down on my anger.
D. Never be bitter toward you.
E. Hold our marriage bed undefiled.

IV.

Mal 2:14
John 15:13
Prov 31:12
1 Cor 13:7
Prov 17:7
Rom 12:10
Prov 5:19

Look at you as my wife by covenant.

A. Call you my friend so I will lay my life down for you at all times.
B. Trust you.
C. Believe the best about you at all times.
D. Be a friend who loves you at all times.
E. Devote myself to you in phileo—brotherly—love and give preference to you in honor.
F. Be intoxicated always by your love.

People of Destiny, a bimonthly magazine edited by Larry Tomczak, is for Christians who know they have a vital part to play in reaching this world for Jesus Christ. If that's you, *People of Destiny* magazine is a tool for your hands. It tackles those tough issues you need to know.

- discover your gifts and fulfill your ministry;
- overcome sinful habits and live victoriously;
- become more effective and disciplined in prayer and Bible study;
- develop strong committed relationships;
- believe God for signs and wonders to confirm the preaching of his Word;
- speak out with conviction on the moral issues of our day;
- learn how to play a vital part in the restoration of New Testament Christianity and the evangelization of the world.

"You can discover your destiny in life! Our commitment to help you is not simply a preference; it's a passion!"
—Larry Tomczak